THE ARCHAEOLOGY OF SOMERSET

EDITED BY CHRIS WEBSTER & TOM MAYBERRY

First Published in Great Britain in 2007

British Library Cataloguing-in-Publication Data
A CIP record for this title is available from the British Library

ISBN 978 0 86183 437 2

SOMERSET BOOKS
Official Publisher to Somerset County Council

Halsgrove House
Ryelands Farm Industrial Estate
Bagley Green
Wellington
Somerset TA21 9PZ
Call: 01823 653777
Fax: 01823 665294
Email: sales@halsgrove.com
Website: www.halsgrove.com

Designed by Lawrence Bostock
Somerset County Council Heritage Service

Printed and bound by D'Auria Industrie Grafiche Spa, Italy

Front cover: Approaching Cadbury Castle in the 5th century AD, by Jane Brayne

Back cover: Detail from the Low Ham mosaic

Overleaf: The Ruins of Glastonbury Abbey, c. 1810 by George Arnold (1763-1841). Arnold shows the ruins in a highly romanticized way, and enhances the pictorial effect by moving not only the Lady Chapel, but also the Abbot's Kitchen and even Glastonbury Tor.

CONTENTS

Contributors

Talya Bagwell is Historic Environment Record Officer, Somerset Heritage Service

Richard Brunning is the Heritage Officer for the Somerset Levels and Moors, Somerset Heritage Service

Robert Croft is the County Archaeological Officer, Somerset Heritage Service

David Dawson was formerly head of the Somerset County Museum Service and is now a heritage consultant

Tom Mayberry is County Heritage Officer, Somerset Heritage Service

Stephen Minnitt is head of the Somerset County Museums, Somerset Heritage Service

Brian Murless has been an active member of the Somerset Industrial Archaeology Society for many years

Chris Norman has been studying early human occuption for many years and has recently completed a PhD

Chris Webster is Historic Environment Record Manager, Somerset Heritage Service

FOREWORD

BY PROFESSOR MICK ASTON

It is now more than thirty years since I arrived in Somerset as the County Council's first Field Archaeologist. They were exciting times. The M5 Motorway had just cut a swathe through the county, disrupting landscapes that had been settled and farmed for thousands of years. Professional archaeologists, together with an army of volunteers, struggled to record the wealth of archaeology that emerged as a result. That was also the period when the work of the archaeologist finally gained acceptance as an essential part of the planning process, and when landscape archaeology emerged strongly as a discipline in its own right. As a landscape archaeologist myself, I have lived happily with the consequences of that fact ever since.

Somerset thirty years ago was still a place where you could make really important discoveries just by looking over a hedge. I well remember the summer evening in 1976 when I climbed a gate in south Somerset and found myself confronted by an amazing sea of earthworks. I had just discovered Nether Adber, one of the county's best-preserved deserted medieval villages. Somerset has been rich in other discoveries and new research since that time, and it is a real pleasure to welcome this splendidly illustrated book. It brings our knowledge up to date, and does so in a way that is both scholarly and accessible. It also reflects new areas of enquiry, such as the archaeology of the Second World War, which have come to prominence since the publication of the last overview of Somerset archaeology (Aston and Burrow 1982).

Over the past fifteen years the popularity of archaeology through television and the media has increased enormously. Somerset County Council has played a key part in that through its involvement in numerous Time Team programmes at such places as Athelney (1993 and again in 2003) and at Dinnington and Charterhouse with the Big Roman Dig in 2005. Archaeological stories are often front-page news and I know that Somerset has a great deal more to offer.

Whether you know a lot about the subject or very little, this is sure to be a book which informs and surprises you, as it uncovers part of the rich and complex past of a county like no other.

5

The Roman mosaic from Low Ham, now preserved in the Somerset County Museum, Taunton. The mosaic dates from the mid 4th century AD and depicts the story of Dido and Aeneas as told by the Roman poet Virgil.

The History of Archaeology in Somerset

A sense of the past

Human awareness of the past can be glimpsed as far back as 2000 years ago. Artefacts recovered during excavation of the Iron Age lake villages at Glastonbury and Meare included items from earlier periods such as Neolithic stone axes and leaf-shaped arrowheads. These items must have been brought from elsewhere though the motive for their collection is unclear. Superstition, personal gain or simple curiosity are among the possible explanations.

Later, in the Roman period, there is evidence that Bronze Age round barrows were investigated, probably in a search for grave goods. When Wick Barrow, Stogursey, was excavated in 1907 the primary burial and grave goods were missing, removed by robbers who conveniently lost a coin dating to around AD 340. Later people occasionally re-used earlier Roman artefacts. At least two graves excavated at Cannington cemetery had Roman coins placed within them, one of them pierced for use as a pendant. More unusually, a broken Roman antler hoe was found in a medieval quarry in Shapwick. One suggestion is that the hoe was a chance find recovered in the Middle Ages during stone robbing of a Roman ruin.

As well as the collection and reuse of physical items from the past, monuments became associated with folklore. A past was fabricated, showing an awareness of the passage

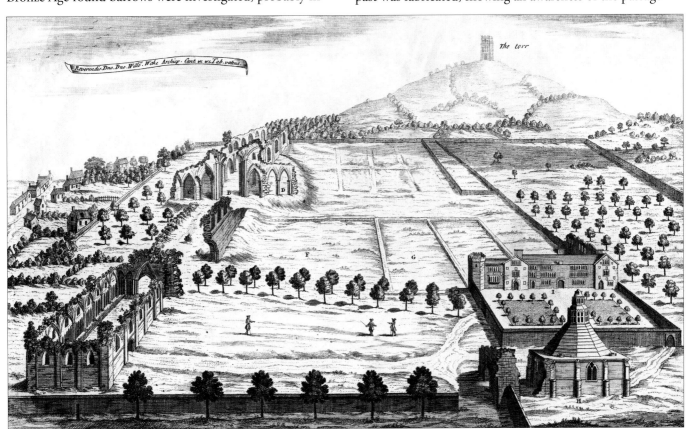

William Stukeley's view, published in 1724, of the ruins of Glastonbury Abbey with the Tor in the background. The ruins of the Medieval abbey are much as we see them today, but the house to the right, incorporating the Late Medieval Abbot's Lodging, has now gone and has been little studied in comparison to the abbey.

of time and a need to understand what had gone before. There are many instances of fanciful stories attached to such monuments in Somerset. Stones at Battlegore, Williton, probably from a chambered tomb, are said to have resulted from a stone-throwing contest between the devil and a giant. Robin Hood's Butts, a group of round barrows in the parish of Otterford, are reputedly the result of giants throwing heaps of earth at one another. Cow Castle, a hillfort of Iron-Age date on Exmoor, is claimed to be a fairy stronghold, built to withstand dangerous earth spirits.

EARLY ANTIQUARIANS

Out of the murkiness of legend a more serious interest in the past developed from the Tudor period onwards. Amongst the foremost of Tudor antiquaries was the scholar and royal librarian John Leland who travelled across England in the 1530s and 40s. His *Itinerary* is an account of his journeys and includes descriptions of some of the sites he saw. Leland made at least three visits to Somerset between 1535 and 1543 and recorded sites at Wells, Evercreech, Bruton, Castle Cary, North and South Cadbury, Ilchester, Montacute and Stoke sub Hamdon. Other early antiquarian visitors to the county included the 16th-century Oxford scholar William Camden and the 17th-century researcher William Stukeley. Stukeley's legacy includes a number of drawings, such as those of Glastonbury Abbey and of Cadbury Castle published in 1724.

In 1791 the first major, countywide survey appeared with the publication in three volumes of *The History and Antiquities of the County of Somerset* by John Collinson. The work includes descriptions and interpretations of sites across the county. Though simplistic in approach by today's standards, Collinson's *History* represents an important stage on the route to understanding the county's past.

In the 18th and 19th centuries interest in the past often focused on round barrows and, more specifically, their contents. Depressions still visible in the centre of many of the county's barrows bear witness to the age of the 'barrow digger'. Occasionally serious attempts were made

to understand these monuments but, sadly for modern researchers, in the majority of cases the aim was the quick retrieval of objects. The barrow diggers tended to be men of relatively high social standing and education with the means and connections to access such sites. Local labourers usually undertook the physical work, often with an audience of invited guests.

John Skinner, rector of Camerton from 1800 to 1839, was especially active and, employing miners from the North Somerset coalfield, he opened many barrows on Mendip. Skinner's approach was to mark out an area on the top of a barrow where the men were instructed to dig downwards until near the bottom of the mound, at which point they were to send for him. On one occasion six barrows were dug in a single afternoon. Skinner's methods were woefully inadequate by modern standards, but he did keep records, both written and drawn, which have survived. Many of the artefacts retrieved have also survived in local museum collections.

Richard Fenton (1747–1821), a Welsh-born lawyer, author and contemporary of John Skinner, made a brief visit to West Somerset in 1807, later publishing his experiences as *A Barrister's Tour through Somerset*. During his stay he too employed labourers to dig into a number of barrows and said that through 'constant experience [they] are deeply skilled in the operation'. On 1 November two or three barrows were opened on Selworthy Beacon, where only charcoal was recovered. The following day four barrows were investigated at Dunkery Beacon. Although results were disappointing in terms of finds, and weather conditions were poor, Fenton's enthusiasm for 'these stupendous mounds of stone raised, as my fancy suggested, over chiefs who had merited highly of their country' was not dampened. 'I am fairly bit, and have the barrow mania strongly on me.' The knowledge gained by this particular kind of investigation does not, perhaps, make up for the damage done.

Roman remains were another focus of interest. Sites often included well-preserved structural elements and excavation, or 'wall-chasing', was popular. In the 1820s

Samuel and Nathanial Buck's drawing of Dunster Castle in 1733. Drawings such as this provide important evidence of the castle before the Victorian restorations.

Lithograph by Samuel Hassell showing a mosaic found at Pitney in 1828. Often, illustrations of the pavement are all that was recorded of early Roman villa excavations - and in some cases even the location of the site is now lost.

and 30s the local antiquarian Samuel Hasell investigated sites in the Somerton area, including at Littleton, Charlton Mackrell, Hurcot and Pitney. The villa at Pitney, one of a number in the parish, was the most thoroughly explored and produced three mosaics. Although Hasell's methods were relatively poor, a summary of his results was published in 1832 by his friend and collaborator Sir Richard Colt Hoare.

LEARNED SOCIETIES & THE FIRST PROFESSIONALS

The informal network of individual antiquarians was partially formalised in 1849 with the founding of the Somerset Archaeological and Natural History Society. For the first 50 years of its existence the Society's interest was primarily focused on historical and topographical Somerset, with a particular emphasis on castles, churches and monasteries. Nevertheless, some chance archaeological discoveries were published, including a hoard of Bronze Age metalwork from Edington Burtle in 1854, Roman pottery kilns at Shepton Mallet in 1864, and the probably

6th-century inscription on the Caratacus stone, Exmoor, in 1890. In 1880 C W Dymond published a description of the Abbot's Way, the first real attempt to record and interpret a prehistoric timber trackway, and in 1896 F T Elworthy recorded a Beaker burial found inside a stone cist at Culbone during quarrying for road stone.

The Society was instrumental in ensuring the preservation of a number of the county's archaeological sites at a time when no official legislation existed (the Monuments Protection Act was not passed until 1882). In the 1850s a contribution of sixteen shillings was made towards the cost of remedial works to Stoney Littleton long barrow and in 1874 the Society purchased and began the renovation of Taunton Castle, subsequently used as their headquarters, library and museum. The Society's collections still form the basis of the extensive reference collections cared for today by the Somerset County Museums Service.

Arguably the first large-scale excavations of high standard in Somerset were those conducted by a local man, Arthur Bulleid (1862–1951), on the site of the Glastonbury Lake Village. Bulleid discovered the site in 1892 after searching for four years for Somerset parallels to the then recently-reported Swiss lake villages. The site was first noticed as a series of low mounds in wetland to the west of Glastonbury where examination of molehills revealed pottery and animal bones. Bulleid quickly received permission to investigate further and soon confirmed his belief that the Somerset wetlands would yield a lake village. Occupied in the later Iron Age, the settlement provided an unparalleled insight into the period. Indeed for some decades afterwards it was the type-site for the British Iron Age.

Bulleid had received no formal training in archaeological excavation but his concern for recording details and in using a multi-disciplinary approach was highly advanced for its time and rarely matched by his contemporaries. In his spare time Bulleid also worked for many years at Meare Lake Village, and other research included Neolithic long barrows of north Somerset as well as the excavation of a Roman villa at Keynsham.

In 1901 a new personality appeared on the scene when

The Culbone cist shortly after its discovery during quarrying in 1896.

Harold St George Gray was appointed Museum Curator and Assistant Secretary of the Somerset Archaeological and Natural History Society. Gray gained his early experience on the archaeological staff of the renowned excavator General Pitt-Rivers, rising from fourth assistant in 1888 to chief assistant and secretary by 1899. Having received perhaps the best archaeological training then available, Gray arrived in the county as an ambitious man keen to make his mark. He quickly became involved in a series of excavations, his earliest being in 1902 at Glastonbury Lake Village. Together with Bulleid, Gray returned to the site annually between 1904 and 1907 and eventually completed its total excavation. In common with earlier work, agricultural labourers undertook most of the strenuous physical digging.

Hardly a year passed during Gray's 48-year tenure as Curator when he did not undertake one or more excavations. Meare Lake Village was the subject of his most prolonged investigation. Excavation commenced there in 1908 and the final season ended in1956 when Gray was aged 86. He carried out a number of more modest excavations on a wide variety of sites around the county, including Bronze Age round barrows at Battlegore (Williton), Combe Beacon (Combe St Nicholas), Wick

Members of the Somerset Archaeological and Natural History Society at Glastonbury Abbey in 1902. Until the Second World War the Society's annual meeting lasted three days and was based in a different part of the county each year.

Arthur Bulleid (in the doorway) and Harold St George Gray (right) on the site of Meare Lake Village in 1935. With them are the Poet Laureate John Masefield (left) and Abbot Ethelbert Horne of Downside Abbey.

left: Interior of the site hut used by Arthur Bulleid and Harold St George Gray during the Meare Lake Village excavations. This reconstruction can be seen in the site hut itself at the Peat Moors Centre, Westhay.

Barrow (Stogursey) and the stone circle at Porlock. Hillforts were a particular interest and investigations were undertaken at Norton Camp (Norton Fitzwarren), Cadbury Castle (South Cadbury), Small Down Camp (Evercreech), Kingsdown Camp (Mells) and Ham Hill (Stoke sub Hamdon). Medieval sites included Taunton Castle, Burrow Mump and Castle Neroche. Many of Gray's excavations were published in the Society's *Proceedings* whilst others appeared in national journals. Unfortunately some, notably Taunton Castle, were never fully published. Gray's other contribution was in enriching the collections of the museum. Artefacts were recovered through Gray's own excavations as well as wider procurement activities around the country and across the world.

Smaller societies, with more specific research interests and geographical coverage, were also evolving in this period. In the north of the county, the Bristol Spelaeological Society began life in 1912 with the intention of studying all aspects of caves in a scientific manner. One of their first archaeological projects was the excavation of Aveline's Hole, Burrington Combe, where the importance of the finds led to the society reforming under the auspices of the University of Bristol. The society continues today with the aims of 'the discovery of caves and the examination of their contents'.

One of the leading lights of the early years of the society was E K Tratman (d. 1978), who joined in 1919 and rose to become president in the 1960s. As well as exploring and recording many cave systems and sites, Tratman also published on such diverse archaeological topics as barrows (which he catalogued), stone circles, henges and Roman remains. H E Balch (1869–1958) was another pioneer of cave exploration on Mendip and excavated at Chelm's Combe Cave near Cheddar Gorge and also at Wookey Hole. Balch was active in the Wells Archaeological and Natural History Society along with A T Wicks (1880–1960). Wicks had a particular interest in Mendip barrows and concentrated much effort on the manuscripts of John Skinner, attempting to locate accurately the sites described and excavated over a hundred years earlier.

Excavations at the southern end of Glastonbury Lake Village in 1897.

MODERN PIONEERS

The most prolific student of Somerset barrows was Leslie Grinsell (1907–1995). In 1936 Grinsell produced *The Ancient Burial Mounds of England*, the first serious attempt to catalogue the numbers, types and distribution of barrows in England. Grinsell was Keeper of Archaeology at Bristol City Museum between 1952 and 1972 and from here journeyed by public transport all over southern England to produce a series of county studies of barrows, including those of Berkshire, Devon, Dorset, Gloucestershire, Hampshire, the Isle of Wight, Surrey, Sussex and Wiltshire. It is estimated that during the course of his career Grinsell recorded over 10,000 barrows, each carefully measured by pacing. Grinsell's survey of Somerset barrows was published by the Somerset Archaeological and Natural History Society in two parts (1961–2), the ninth county survey to be completed. Grinsell aimed to visit every site listed and combined this fieldwork with thorough documentary research, including Skinner's manuscripts as well as Anglo-Saxon boundary charters, which often referred to barrows. Grinsell also became interested in the folklore associated with barrows and collected stories about them.

Elsewhere in the county attention was focused on the active investigation of important ecclesiastical sites. The late 19th century had seen many ambitious, and often destructive, restoration programmes coupled with research on the physical remains of churches, chapels and disused structures. Abandoned sites, such as monasteries, became popular for their picturesque appeal and ruins were often altered to increase their scenic qualities.

Ralegh Radford's excavations in the Great Hall of Taunton Castle in 1952, which he undertook with the assistant museum keeper, A D Hallam. They showed that the Great Hall had originally been a much shorter, but wider, building; the scars of its vaulted roof are visible in the wall in the background.

Although early work tended to concentrate on architectural and historical elements, excavation was also undertaken. Athelney Abbey was excavated in 1872, Muchelney between 1872 and 1874, and Glastonbury Abbey saw rapid initial excavation by W J St John Hope in 1904. Subsequently thirty-six seasons of digging, between 1908 and 1979, were undertaken at Glastonbury in the name of the Society of Antiquaries of London and the Somerset Archaeological and Natural History Society. More than fifty percent of the known extent of the abbey complex was excavated but little detail has been published. The first director was the noted architect F Bligh Bond who excavated between 1908 and 1922. In spite of solid recording techniques Bond is often more remembered for his later love of non-scientific research methods, including automatic writing, which led to his scandalous dismissal in 1922. Another renowned excavator of Glastonbury Abbey was C A Ralegh Radford (1900–1998) who worked on the site between 1951 and 1963 and was most interested in Saxon and potentially earlier remains.

The earlier 20th century was also the time in which a desire to understand the archaeology of the county as a synthesized whole, rather than a collection of disparate sites and separate time periods, became apparent. *The Archaeology of Somerset*, an overview of the county's known pre-Norman archaeology edited by Dinah Dobson (later Dina Dobson-Hinton), was published in 1931. Dobson's first husband was an early president of the University of Bristol Spelaeological Society and the content of the book reflects this association, having an emphasis on cave sites and prehistory. In 1965 Leslie Grinsell published an article entitled 'Somerset archaeology, 1931–65' detailing knowledge acquired since the appearance of Dobson's book. The article not only provided new information on long-studied areas and periods but also explored previously-neglected themes, as in the section by Neil Cossons on industrial archaeology.

While eminent professional archaeologists were recording and synthesizing knowledge, a number of keen amateurs, with specific research interests, were amassing important collections. In the west of the county, for example, A L Wedlake (1900–1990) was collecting and studying flint work collected along the coastal area between Porlock and Kilve. Wedlake had started to collect flints while working on his land in the 1930s and from small beginnings he went on to amass one of the most extensive lithic collections in the South West. Wedlake's work led not only to the acquisition of new artefacts for study but also to the identification of some important sites. In 1942, for example, he discovered a lithic scatter at Hawkcombe Head on Exmoor, which proved to be Late Mesolithic in date and is still being researched.

Samuel Nash (1913–1985), the Surrey-born son of a postman, occupied his spare time in the pursuit of the past of Highbridge and surrounding areas. He was a keen visitor to holes being dug for any purpose, as well as a thorough documentary researcher. Between 1955, when he moved to the area, and his death in 1985 he visited hundreds of sites recording features and artefacts found. Although his interest at the time focused on the Roman period, Nash collected important information on later sites as well as recording places where no evidence was found, useful information for the modern planner. In addition to his monitoring activities Nash was also instrumental in founding the Burnham on Sea Archaeological and Natural History Society, under whose auspices a number of small excavations were undertaken. In 1971, towards the end of his active archaeological investigations, he was asked to become involved in recording work prior to the construction of the M5 motorway, a testament to his skills and reputation.

The second half of the 20th century saw the growth of professional archaeology in Somerset. Foremost among the early professionals was Philip Rahtz who had become acquainted with the archaeologist Ernest Greenfield while serving in the RAF. Friendship with Greenfield sparked a personal interest in archaeology and later a professional career which began with their excavations at Chew Valley Lake in 1953. Rahtz memorably described excavating on an island that grew smaller each day as the water rose in the newly-constructed reservoir.

In 1960–2 Rahtz returned to Somerset and excavated at Cheddar, in advance of the construction of a new school, discovering the Saxon and medieval royal palace later used by the bishops of Bath and Wells. In the following years he also undertook excavations at the important post-Roman cemetery at Cannington, threatened by quarrying. In the mid-1960s a revival of interest in King Arthur led to excavations at sites associated with the legends, namely Glastonbury, long believed to be the isle of Avalon, and South Cadbury, which the locals had told John Leland was the site of Camelot. Rahtz was employed by the Chalice Well Trust between 1964–6 to excavate on the summit of the Tor, where he was able to demonstrate the presence of timber structures in the 6th century with evidence of associated metalworking. The site later developed into an outpost of the abbey. Following this success Rahtz excavated other sites in the Glastonbury area, including Beckery Chapel and Chalice Well itself.

At South Cadbury, the identification of the site as Camelot had been reinforced when pottery sherds had been recognised as 6th-century imports of a type first identified at Tintagel in Cornwall. This led to the founding of the Camelot Research Committee, which appointed the Cardiff academic Leslie Alcock (1925–2006) as excavation director. Large-scale excavations ran from 1966 to 1970 with a further short season in 1973. This work recorded the earthwork defences of the hillfort and developed one of the most complete ceramic sequences in the country, covering the period from the Late Bronze Age to the end of the Iron Age. It was evidence of the site's post-Roman reuse, however, that most caught the imagination of the public and the archaeological world. As well as discovering extensive new defences, the plans of timber buildings were recovered with high-status finds that showed a higher degree of social organisation than had previously been imagined. Work continues through the endeavours of the South Cadbury Environs Project, a landscape survey initiated in 1998.

Leslie Alcock (left) discussing the excavations at South Cadbury with Sir Mortimer Wheeler and one of his students. The site, with its Arthurian connections, generated a huge public interest that funded much of the site work.

THE M5 AND AFTER

Large-scale development in the 1960s and 70s highlighted the dangers to which archaeological remains were subject and led to the formation of organisations to undertake 'rescue archaeology'. In 1969 the proposed construction of the M5 motorway through Gloucestershire, Bristol and Somerset led to the formation of the M5 Research Committee, chaired by Peter Fowler of Bristol Universty. The project received little public funding and relied heavily on voluntary effort. The experiences of those pioneers, co-ordinating archaeological fieldwork of an unprecedented scale in the path of a major construction project, had a number of important consequences for archaeology, both within the region and nationally. Archaeology gained vital recognition as a valid consideration within the planning process, the M5 project providing a model for archaeological response to large-scale development that was to be emulated in a number of subsequent road-building schemes. The work also led to the growth of landscape archaeology as a discipline and a realisation of the great time-scales represented by the archaeology of our surroundings.

Another response to large-scale development was the creation of CRAAGS (the Committee for Rescue Archaeology in Avon, Gloucestershire and Somerset), established in 1973 and funded by grants from central government. CRAAGS carried out many small excavations in Somerset together with larger campaigns during redevelopment in Taunton and, particularly, around Ilchester. In parallel with this Somerset County Council employed Mick Aston in its Planning Department to assess the archaeological potential of development sites. As part of his work Aston established a 'Sites and Structures Record' recording the whereabouts of archaeological sites. This has now evolved to become a vast repository of information on the archaeological sites, activities, listed buildings, and other historic elements of the county. Available online since 2003, it is now known as Somerset's 'Historic Environment Record', and has become a vital tool for education, research and planning.

The Somerset Levels Project in the Brue Valley was another major initiative born out of the need to record a vanishing resource. In 1970, peat extraction uncovered a prehistoric wooden trackway that had aroused the interest of John Coles at Cambridge University. Although trackways and worked wood had been found before, the Sweet Track (named after the finder, Ray Sweet) proved to be of Neolithic date and large-scale excavations started in 1973. The techniques developed over the fifteen years of the project were highly innovative and form the basis of wetland archaeology as practised across the world.

The importance of studies of whole landscapes, rather than individual sites, continues to be recognised across the county and a number of large-scale projects have been undertaken. On high ground such as the Quantock Hills and Exmoor aerial photographic interpretation has been combined with ground survey to understand a complex landscape developed through thousands of years of occupation and use. The Shapwick Project, initiated by Mick Aston and Bristol University, has investigated all elements of this 'typical English village' within a landscape context using a multitude of archaeological techniques combined with thorough documentary research. The project ran throughout the 1990s and also provided a valuable training exercise for students of Bristol and Winchester universities.

John Coles, co-director of the Somerset Levels Project.

Another significant trend in the county in recent decades is an increasing interest in the physical elements of the very recent past, many constructed within living memory. A significant and growing body of knowledge continues to be collected on 20th-century defensive structures such as pillboxes and airfields, as well as associated military accommodation and transport infrastructure. Research also continues into Somerset's industrial past, pursued most actively by the Somerset Industrial Archaeology Society.

The establishment of a national Portable Antiquities Scheme, for which Somerset acted as a pilot area in 1997, is another new element in archaeological research in the county. Funding has been provided to encourage the voluntary recording of artefacts found by members of the public. The scheme has certainly raised awareness of the importance of recording chance finds and also aims to promote responsible methods of collecting, so maximising the information gained and minimising potential damage to both artefacts and sites. The local Finds Liaison Officers are based at Somerset County Museum.

Today, there is more archaeological work in the county than ever before, mostly funded by developers and carried out by professional archaeological contractors. Somerset County Council coordinates this activity, through the development control sections of the District Councils, and sets standards for the work. Much of the work is small-scale, but there are more extensive projects on road schemes and large developments such as the Mendip Business Park on the site of the Roman town of Shepton Mallet. The results of smaller projects are often not formally published but they can be consulted at the Somerset Record Office and on the Historic Environment Record, which also contains many of the results of the continuing endeavours of amateur archaeologists who maintain the tradition begun by John Skinner over 200 years ago.

The County Archaeologist, Bob Croft (left), and Steve Minnitt of the Somerset County Museum (centre) discuss progress with Mick Aston during filming for Time Team at Dinnington Roman villa.

Palaeolithic and Mesolithic

Introduction

Somerset is fortunate in having a wide range of evidence for early human activity. From the first confirmed traces of hominids in England around half a million years ago to the disappearance of the last hunter-gathering groups some 6000 to 5500 years ago, this period represents over 98% of the time humans are known to have been present in northern Europe. Current research into this remote period is progressing rapidly and should produce some exciting results over the next few years. Already some archaeologists have suggested that the initial occupation of southern England could have taken place even earlier, during an episode of warm climate that occurred around 700,000 years ago.

The results of recent scientific research have greatly enhanced our understanding of the climate and environment of western Europe during this long period. It is becoming clear that a complex, cyclical pattern of climatic change has taken place. Several major cold or glacial stages have been identified, alternating with warm or interglacial stages when mean annual temperatures were similar to or slightly above those of today. Between these two extremes were long intervals of generally cool climate, with occasional short-lived milder episodes (known as interstadials).

Inevitably, these frequent and often dramatic shifts in climate had far-reaching effects on the environment and ecology of north-western Europe. With cool conditions prevailing during most of this period, a greater proportion of the Earth's surface water was locked into ice sheets than is the case today. As a result, world sea levels were, for the most part, lower than at present and southern England was joined to the European mainland by a broad river valley now occupied by the English Channel. At the onset of each interglacial stage, however, the large-scale melting of ice led to a rapid rise in sea level, resulting in the flooding of coastal plains and valleys. In this way, Britain became an offshore island on at least four occasions prior to the present warm stage.

There is increasing evidence to suggest that warm interglacial conditions were heralded by a sharp rise in mean annual temperature. In southern England, the open landscape of the preceding cold stage would have been rapidly colonised by temperate woodlands, which soon developed into full deciduous forest. As the climate deteriorated following the peak of each interglacial, these forests gave way to more open conditions and finally to a cool, sub-arctic flora. Animal populations ebbed and flowed in response to these changes with temperate woodland species migrating southwards out of Britain as the forests retreated, to be replaced by others better adapted to cooler, more open environments. During the most severe cold episodes southern England became a very inhospitable place, with little vegetation and only a limited, cold-adapted fauna.

Until the present warm stage, which began about 10,000 years ago, southern England was often a marginal area both in terms of its location and its occasionally harsh environment. As human survival depended largely on meat and fat as sources of food, animal migrations into and out of the region would have played a key role in determining whether or not human groups were present at any given time.

The Lower Palaeolithic
(before 500,000 to about 250,000 years ago)

During the long Lower Palaeolithic period, Somerset was occupied intermittently by groups of early humans, the more recent of whom were probably the ancestors of the Neanderthals. These highly mobile hominids probably survived by hunting, scavenging meat from predator kills and foraging for roots, nuts and other edible material. They made a limited range of stone tools including the hand-axe, which was an efficient butchery and general purpose cutting implement. Although finds of hand-axes are fairly widespread in Somerset, only at a site near Westbury sub Mendip can any archaeological evidence be assigned to a specific climatic stage with any confidence.

In 1969, traces of an ancient infilled cave were discovered in a limestone quarry high on the Mendip escarpment above Westbury sub Mendip. As quarrying progressed, a 100-metre-wide cross-section through this feature was exposed in the quarry face, revealing layers of sand and gravel overlain by a series of fossil-rich cave sediments. Working under very difficult conditions, various investigators have obtained numerous bones and teeth of now-extinct animals including a sabre-toothed cat, a jaguar, an early rhinoceros and several species of vole. Recent work, on the abundant vole remains discovered, has indicated that the sediments were formed during an interglacial stage that began about 500,000 years ago.

The cave sediments have also produced numerous poorly-preserved flakes and fragments of flint and chert. Many of these are believed to be artefacts and thus could represent early evidence for a human presence in Britain. This appears to be confirmed by recent work at the Natural History Museum, where deliberate cut marks on fossil mammal bone from the site have been identified. What is certain is that the Westbury sub Mendip cave is a site of major significance, both for its abundant fossil fauna and for its potential as an early hominid site.

Elsewhere in Somerset, the evidence for Lower Palaeolithic activity consists almost entirely of surface finds of stone artefacts, mainly handaxes. There is a thin scattering of findspots on the Mendip plateau, around the Quantock Hills and in the Chard and Yeovil areas. Many finds have been made in the Vale of Taunton Deane, where recent fieldwork has produced several hundred artefacts from surface sites at Norton Fitzwarren and Trull. Near the latter village, a major concentration of stone tools and manufacturing waste was located on a hill overlooking Taunton. Here, pieces of Greensand chert from nearby gravel deposits were used to make handaxes, scrapers and other tools, which suggests that this locality could have served as a temporary base for hominid groups who were engaged in procuring food from the adjacent valley.

On the West Somerset coast, over twenty handaxes and a number of flakes have been found on the foreshore between Doniford and St Audries Bay. Although now heavily worn, many of the handaxes are good examples made of Greensand chert, the nearest source of which lies some fifteen miles to the south near Taunton. It seems possible that these were selected tools, carried ready-made into the area by bands of hunter-scavengers who also frequented the southern parts of the county.

These handaxe finds from Somerset are, strictly speaking, undatable. Comparisons with better documented areas such as East Anglia and the Thames valley suggest, however, that the majority may belong to a period between about 425,000 and 300,000 years ago, after which secure evidence for a human presence in southern England becomes increasingly sparse. In Somerset, there is little to suggest any human activity during most of the ensuing Middle Palaeolithic period and it may be that, from around 180,000 years ago until the middle of the most recent (Devensian) cold stage (about 60,000 years ago), the region was totally uninhabited.

above: *Lower Palaeolithic handaxe from the Chard area.*

THE LATE MIDDLE PALAEOLITHIC
(ABOUT 60,000 TO 40,000 YEARS AGO)

During the Mid-Devensian, southern England had a cool, dry climate interspersed with many brief episodes of both milder and colder conditions. For much of this period, wide expanses of rich, arid grassland supported herds of mammoth, giant deer and horse in addition to woolly rhinoceros and a range of carnivore species. It was into this environment, probably around 60,000 years ago, that humans of Neanderthal type arrived, possibly having followed the migrations of animal herds into Britain from the south. Amongst the equipment used by these hunting groups was a range of stone flake tools and a distinctive type of small triangular handaxe.

Cave sites such as those at Uphill near Weston super Mare and at Wookey Hole have produced some evidence of occupation during this period. Unfortunately, these sites were discovered during the early days of archaeology, when excavation techniques were relatively crude and the recording of finds was, at best, imprecise.

At Wookey Hole, a tiny cave known as the Hyaena Den lies near the closed end of a steep-sided box ravine, providing an ideal location for observing and trapping wild animals. Recent work here has shown that the driest and sunniest part of the cave entrance was occupied by a small band of Neanderthals, who left behind traces of fire, flake tools and a few small handaxes. Although locally-obtained chert was used to produce sharp flakes, some

Woolly mammoths were part of the rich fauna that roamed Somerset during the Devensian cold stage. Inset is a drawing of a lion's skull found at Sandford Hill and dating to a warm stage.

19

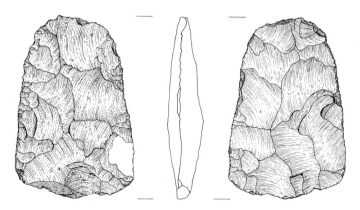

Palaeolithic hunters at the Hyaena Den, Wookey Hole.

Den closely resemble finds from the now-destroyed Uphill Cave 8, some 23km to the north-west. It has recently been suggested that both locations might have been used by the same human group, possibly during hunting trips along the foot of the Mendip Hills.

Elsewhere in Somerset, clear signs of Late Middle Palaeolithic activity are restricted to a few isolated finds of small triangular handaxes, the most convincing examples coming from the edge of the Quantocks at North Petherton and West Quantoxhead. These may indicate no more than occasional brief visits to the area during this period.

THE UPPER PALAEOLITHIC (ABOUT 35,000 TO 10,000 YEARS AGO)

At four cave sites on Mendip, evidence has been found for brief occupation by Early Upper Palaeolithic hunters towards the end of the Mid-Devensian, probably between 35,000 and 30,000 years ago. This was a period of sharply oscillating climate, with short cool episodes lasting up to one thousand years interspersed with a number of milder interstadials. For most of this time, extensive dry grasslands with only limited tree growth supported a rich fauna that included mammoth, woolly rhinoceros and hyaena. At the Badger Hole (Wookey Hole) a collection of about twenty flint artefacts thought to date from this period contains four leaf-shaped points, which were probably hafted as spear heads. Bearing a close resemblance to leaf points recorded from central Europe, it has recently been suggested that these pieces could have been

of the handaxes were made of flint and were probably carried some distance to the cave as finished tools. A cut-marked tooth of red deer believed to be associated with this occupation has been radiocarbon dated to around 40,000 years ago. Many of the stone tools from the Hyaena

Early Upper Palaeolithic flint leaf points from Soldier's Hole, Cheddar Gorge.

Distinctive Late Middle Palaeolithic handaxe found at North Petherton.

*Aerial view of Cheddar Gorge.
The caves in the sides of the gorge have
produced some of the best evidence for
Upper Palaeolithic activity in Britain.*

*Pierced shaft of reindeer antler found at Gough's Cave, Cheddar,
possibly used for straightening wooden arrow shafts. Note the parallel
scratch marks which could be decoration or some form of notation.*

made by some of the last groups of Neanderthal-type humans to enter Britain.

The earliest clear evidence for modern-type humans in Somerset comes from Uphill Cave 8, which has produced part of a spear tip made of bone or antler. A radiocarbon date has indicated that this piece is probably between 29,000 and 27,000 years old. It appears to have come from a type of tool associated with the first physically modern humans to enter north-western Europe, probably some time after 35,000 years ago.

After about 25,000 years ago, the climate of north-western Europe grew increasingly cold and, by about 20,000 years ago, the region was in the grip of full glacial conditions. Southern England became an almost barren arctic desert and may have been uninhabited for several thousand years. Conditions improved around 13,000 years ago, when a dramatic rise in temperature initiated the brief warm episode known as the Windermere interstadial. Although winters remained cool and dry, temperatures during the summer months may have been similar to those of today. Both birch woodlands and grassland habitats were present during this period, supporting a fauna that included mammoth, horse, red deer and wild cattle.

It was during this interstadial, shortly after 13,000 years ago, that groups of Late Upper Palaeolithic hunters began entering Britain from the continent. Of the several Mendip caves that were occupied at this time, Gough's Cave in Cheddar Gorge is the most informative. Early excavations here produced large quantities of artefacts and animal bones, including human remains, but these were poorly recorded. More recent studies, including small excavations by staff of the Natural History Museum, have produced a clearer picture of activities at this site.

A series of radiocarbon dates from Gough's Cave suggests that episodes of occupation probably took place over several hundred years. Analysis of pollen from the cave sediments has indicated that, at that time, the climate was drier than today. Whilst in some sheltered spots some woodland may have been able to flourish, the exposed Mendip plateau would probably have been a more open landscape with grasses and dwarf shrubs.

The stone artefacts found included many long, parallel-sided blades of flint. Some of these had been trimmed into so-called Cheddar points, which were probably used as spear tips or knives. There were also scrapers for preparing animal skins, chisel-like burins for working bone and awls for piercing hides. More unusual finds included three perforated shafts of reindeer antler of uncertain function, several bone needles and awls and two possible javelin heads of mammoth ivory. A few pieces of bone and ivory bear roughly parallel marks arranged in groups. These seem to indicate some form of notation, perhaps for use as a tally or for recording the passage of time.

Among the remains of animals hunted or trapped, horse was particularly abundant and red deer, mountain hare, swan and lynx were also present. Many heavily cut-marked bones provide evidence for the careful skinning and butchery of carcasses, including the removal of sinews for use as thongs and snares. The corpses of human adults and children were also subject to careful defleshing and dismemberment. Whether this was part of an elaborate funerary ritual or is an indication of cannibalism is unknown, although the former is perhaps more likely. Whichever was the case, the teeth and bones of at least five individuals ended up mixed with other debris on the floor of the cave.

On balance, it seems possible that Gough's Cave was used as a seasonal base by an extended family group. Occupation may have been intermittent and, during the course of a year, these people may have travelled long distances in pursuit of various resources, including high-quality flint for making blade tools.

After about 12,000 years ago, the later part of the Windermere interstadial is characterised by a drop in average temperatures and the spread of extensive birch woodlands. Apart from the disappearance of the woolly mammoth, the range of animal species present remained largely unchanged and was exploited by hunters whose equipment differed somewhat from the earlier Gough's Cave people. Although known from several parts of

England, evidence suggesting their presence in Somerset is limited to a few finds of typical 'penknife' and curve-backed flint points from the Mendip area.

Following the end of the interstadial around 10,800 years ago, there was a swift return to cold arctic conditions, with reindeer herds once again returning to southern Britain. During the coldest part of this episode, the region may have been uninhabited but, by about 10,200 years ago, hunting groups were again active in England. There is as yet no clear evidence that these people, who appear to have been closely-related to reindeer hunters on the North German plain, penetrated as far west as Somerset.

The Mesolithic
(about 9500 to 5500 years ago)

About 10,000 years ago, the Devensian cold stage was brought to an abrupt end by a rapid rise in temperature. This marked the beginning of the present warm period, known as the Holocene, and it has been estimated that the transition from a sub-arctic to a fully temperate climate could have occurred in less than fifty years. As temperatures rose, southern England was rapidly colonised by birch woodland and, within a thousand years, widespread forests containing hazel, pine and oak were firmly established. This new environment supported a rich fauna including red deer, roe deer, wild cattle and pig.

The Late Devensian hunters of north-western Europe seem to have adapted quickly to their changing environment with a more generalised hunter-gatherer way of life evolving as the variety of natural resources increased. Waterfowl, beaver and fish could have been obtained from rivers and lakes and, from the woodlands, hazel nuts, edible roots and berries would have been available in season. Of the animals hunted, red deer are of particular significance as the short migrations of herds between higher, more open ground in summer and lowland areas in winter may have influenced the movements of the hunter-gatherers, particularly in hilly regions such as Somerset. Unlike their Upper Palaeolithic forebears, however, these Mesolithic groups probably had no need to travel long distances during the course of a year, as forest-dwelling animals tend to be more sedentary than their counterparts in open landscapes.

In the archaeological record, the onset of the Mesolithic period is marked by the appearance of flaked stone axes for working wood, as well as numerous small flint points called microliths, which were probably used as tips and barbs for wooden arrows. In Somerset, undoubted Mesolithic artefacts have been found at over seventy locations, usually in the form of surface scatters that cannot be accurately dated. It is, however, often possible to distinguish early sites, dating to before about 9000 years ago, from later sites by variations in the shapes of stone tools, particularly microliths, which are present.

A large collection of Mesolithic artefacts was obtained from a sand quarry at Greylake, near Middlezoy. Good quality flint and chert was used to make a range of tools including a small axe, chisel-like burins, microliths and numerous scrapers. These tools are typical of the early part of the period and are identical to those from sites elsewhere in England that have been radiocarbon dated to between about 9500 and 9000 years ago. At Greylake, the types of tool present suggest that this may have been a seasonal base camp, possibly occupied during the autumn or winter months. The large number of scrapers present may indicate that the preparation of animal skins, including deer hides, was an important activity here.

On Mendip, there is important evidence for the use of caves as burial places during the Early Mesolithic. At Gough's Cave, Cheddar, the famous skeleton of Cheddar Man, currently on display in the cave museum, has been radiocarbon dated to around 9000 years ago. Between 1797 and 1840, between fifty and a hundred skeletons were excavated from Aveline's Hole in Burrington Combe, although only a few fragments of these now survive. Human remains from a more recent excavation in this cave have yielded a similar radiocarbon date to that obtained for Cheddar Man, suggesting that many, if not all, of the earlier finds may also have been Mesolithic burials. Human remains dated to the Early Mesolithic have also been recovered from cave sites at Badger Hole (Wookey) and

Totty Pot, above Cheddar Gorge.

The majority of Mesolithic find-spots in Somerset have produced artefacts typical of the later part of the period and most are likely to date to after about 7500 years ago. In the Somerset Levels, a large collection of flint and chert artefacts from a site at Chedzoy, near Bridgwater, contains a wide range of tool types, including many tiny triangular and curve-backed microliths typical of the Later Mesolithic. Most of the flint used came from Wiltshire and north Dorset and the occurrence of hollow-based microliths, which may be of somewhat earlier date, suggests links with groups making similar pieces further east in Wessex. It seems possible that the site was occupied intermittently over a long period of time and that, in addition to hunting and foraging, items of equipment and clothing were manufactured or repaired here.

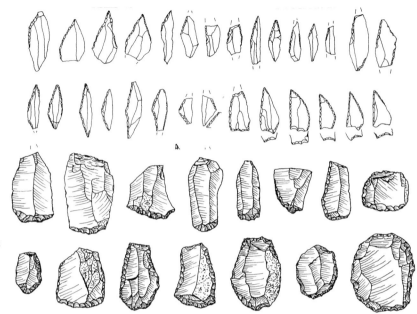

Flint microliths and scrapers from a Mesolithic site at Chedzoy.

Numerous surface finds of Later Mesolithic artefacts have been made on Exmoor, the Quantocks and the Mendip plateau, suggesting that these upland areas were used as hunting grounds, probably during the summer months. Many of these flint scatters are small and may indicate no more than brief camping places.

On Exmoor, many such flint scatters are clustered around the top of a valley overlooking springs at Hawkcombe Head near Porlock. Although the large collections made from here contain numerous microliths, relatively few other standardised tools have been found, which suggests that hunting and gathering activities may have been of prime importance at this location. Although there is currently no evidence for Early Mesolithic activity, the range of microlith shapes present in the collections suggests that episodes of occupation could have taken place over a long period of time.

Apart from a small amount of coloured chert from east Devon, almost all of the artefacts from Hawkcombe Head are made of beach pebble flint, which probably came from the Barnstaple Bay area or further west. This suggests that Later Mesolithic people may have wandered between north Devon and west Somerset, perhaps using inland valley routes or a narrow coastal plain which, at that time, may have fringed the northern edge of Exmoor. Alternatively, beach pebble material could have reached west Somerset through a system of contact and exchange between hunter-gatherer groups. Excavations and fieldwork by the University of Bristol are producing a much clearer picture of Mesolithic activity in the Hawkcombe Head area and, when published, will make an important contribution to our understanding of this period in southern Britain.

The end of the Mesolithic period in Britain has been the subject of much recent discussion. Whilst a few radiocarbon dates suggest that groups with a purely hunter-gatherer way of life may have survived until around 5500 years ago, by this date Neolithic communities practising livestock rearing and crop raising were firmly established in southern England. Thus, in spite of the many theories that have been put forward, the fate of the last hunter-gatherers in Somerset currently remains uncertain.

THE NEOLITHIC

INTRODUCTION

The 1800 years of the Neolithic (*c.* 4000–2200 BC) saw changes in human lifestyle of more significance than anything before or since. At the beginning, groups of people moved seasonally within large territories exploiting the natural resources of different habitats by hunting and gathering. By the end, permanent settlements were the norm, domesticated animals and agricultural crops were the chief source of food, the natural environment was greatly altered to meet human requirements, material culture was diversifying with the introduction of pottery, social stratification and material ostentation were apparent, and great effort was expended in building ritual monuments which served no practical purpose. In short, modern life had begun.

THE CHANGING LANDSCAPE

The environmental information contained within the peat deposits of central Somerset provides us with a good idea of just how radical a change occurred within the Neolithic period. The pollen blown in from the surrounding dryland shows that the area of woodland began to decline and the amount of more open area, represented by grasses or bracken, increased. Some weeds associated with agricultural crops also appear. Farming clearances were sometimes re-colonised by trees but the general trend was for the area of untouched woodland gradually to reduce.

The woods themselves were changing. Before, much of the dryland area had been covered in a dense, high-canopy woodland of oak, lime, elm, ash and hazel. In the Early Neolithic, elm pollen is seen to decline to very low levels. This may have been caused by disease but could also be due to the harvesting of the leaves of the tree for use as a winter fodder crop for domesticated animals. In the areas where farming clearances became reforested, other trees, such as birch which is quick to colonise new areas, became more important and people managed the forms of woodland which developed. The earliest evidence in Great Britain for the use of cow's milk comes from lipids extracted from pottery found beside the Sweet Track (3806 BC).

Wild food would still have formed a very important part of the diet for the early Neolithic period despite the introduction of farming. Even at the end of the Neolithic, hunting mammals, fish and birds was no doubt an important activity, and the collection of nuts and berries would have been a major task in autumn. Bone evidence from sites such as Abbey Quarry, Doulting, includes wild animals such as red deer alongside domestic cattle, sheep and pigs. The gradual nature of the change suggests that there was no sudden influx of a separate farming people, but rather the adoption of new ideas by the existing inhabitants of the area.

The remains of beetles found buried in the peat beside the Sweet Track can give us an idea of what the climate was like in the Neolithic. Four of the species found are now extinct in Britain but still survive in warmer climes on the Continent. This shows that in the Early Neolithic period temperatures were 2–4 degrees colder in winter and 2–3 degrees warmer in summer than they are now. This means that the potential for agricultural activity and settlement was quite different from the present day.

SETTLEMENTS

Unlike on the Continent, very few traces of Neolithic houses have been found in Britain. In Somerset the best evidence for a building comes from a site close to South Cadbury where stake holes and a possible palisade trench defined a compacted house floor. Some other remains were discovered when the A303 was being widened at Maperton Ridge. Here a small collection of post holes, gullies, wall slots, pits and hearths were probably the remains of a Neolithic settlement. Many caves on the edge of Mendip also display evidence of occupation at this time, such as Sun Hole Cave, Soldier's Hole, Outlook Cave and Chelm's Combe Cave at Cheddar. The evidence takes the form of pottery, flint and stone tools and hearths. Caves elsewhere in the county, such as Nettlebridge Cave, Ashwick and Tom Tivey's Hole in Leighton Hanging, also have similar remains.

A combination of pottery, flint and charcoal suggests settlements at some lowland sites such as Edington Burtle, which would then have been a large island in a wet valley. Higher land, such as Ham Hill and Norton (Fitzwarren) Camp, has also produced traces of Neolithic occupation. Neolithic pottery is fragile and, as for earlier periods, the main source of evidence for human settlement and activity comes from flint and stone tools discovered during fieldwalking. Several hundred sites all over the county have been discovered in this way and there are numerous other flint finds that have not been studied in enough detail to ascribe them to a particular period. Many of the find spots, such as those on Ubley Hill Farm at Priddy or Quaking House at Milverton, have yielded hundreds of artefacts. At Monkton Heathfield, Neolithic pottery has been recovered from a substantial ditch, possibly enclosing a settlement.

Very few of these possible occupation sites have ever been excavated, but two are known from South Cadbury. Here a hearth and numerous pits have been discovered both on the top of the hill and beside its south-western foot at Milsom's Corner. The pits contained flint axes, arrowheads and other tools in addition to pottery, hazelnuts and human bones. The exact function of these pits is hard to determine, but it seems clear that what we would see as the distinctions between normal life, ritual activity and disposal of the dead did not exist as they do now.

CEREMONIAL AND DEATH

As well as those from pits at South Cadbury, human remains have also been found scattered among the occupation layers in caves such as Chelm's Combe, Sun Hole and Outlook Cave. This pattern is seen elsewhere in the country where human bones are found in

The wooden 'God Dolly', found under a Neolithic trackway at Westhay, has both male and female characteristics. It was carved over 5000 years ago and is the oldest human figurine discovered in the UK.

ditches, pits and even flint mines. However, some of the Neolithic population were treated in quite a different way at death, and were buried in large ceremonial structures. Long barrows, made chiefly of earth, and long cairns, made principally of stones, are the two most common forms known from Somerset. Such structures sometimes contain stone- or wood-lined chambers or cists containing the unburnt or cremated bones of several individuals, or parts of individuals. Rituals connected with the deposition of human remains in the mound sometimes took place in forecourt areas at one end of the mound.

Reuse over a long period of time is a common feature of such structures. The long barrow destroyed in the landscaping of Fromefield House in the early 19th century produced the bones of over fifteen individuals, and the long barrow at Murtry Hill, Buckland Dinham, contained a stone-lined chamber in which were both unburnt bones and cremations in urns. Areas of burning seen during the excavation of Brimble Pit Pool long barrow, Priddy, suggest that cremations may have taken place in the same location. Excarnation, or exposure of the dead bodies, is believed to be the more frequent treatment of bodies in the British Neolithic.

Only eighteen probable long barrows and one long cairn are known from Somerset. Many have suffered severe damage such as the examples at Whitnell Corner and Pen Hill in the parish of St Cuthbert Out, Wells. The former was damaged by ploughing and the latter was used as a tank obstacle during the Second World War. Most of the surviving examples are now protected as Scheduled Monuments.

The Priddy Circles. Although similar to other henges in Britain, the Priddy Circles are unusual in that the bank lies inside the ditch – a feature shared with Stonehenge. The northernmost circle, which lies on a different alignment, appears not to have been completed.

OTHER RITUAL STRUCTURES

Important ceremonial activities and meetings appear to have taken place within specially defined spaces such as henges or stone circles. Seven henges are known from the county, four of them in one spectacular alignment: the Priddy Circles. These consist of a bank, outside which was a wide ditch, and they range in diameter from 150 to 170m. The bank was made with a core of stone, supported by large posts and small stakes, and capped with the material from the ditch. A causewayed entrance was recorded but neither excavation nor geophysical survey has found anything in the central area. Pollen evidence tells us that the land surrounding the Circles had been cleared of trees and was under grass at the time they were built. The Priddy Circles may have been made one after another, and the northernmost circle remains incomplete.

Cropmarks of many periods at Chedzoy. The rectangular feature (top centre) appears to be the end of a cursus or, possibly, a long mortuary enclosure of Neolithic date. Other features include numerous pits and a circular feature (bottom right) which is probably the ditch of a Bronze Age round barrow. The latest features are field boundaries which seem to be aligned on the barrow – the boundaries disappear where they originally rose up onto the now ploughed-down mound.

Another henge at Gorsey Bigbury, near Cheddar, also revealed a lack of internal features but the excavations did find over 4000 flint tools and waste flakes, and a later Beaker (Early Bronze Age) burial in the ditch accompanied by pottery, flint tools and bone needles. Away from Mendip, aerial photography has located the end of a possible cursus at Chedzoy. This is another type of ritual monument consisting of a linear space defined by banks and ditches. Other ritual activity is evidenced in a series of pits at Abbey Quarry, Doulting, containing antler, worked flint, animal bone and Grooved Ware pottery. Recent excavations at East Lambrook have revealed a causewayed enclosure and a cursus within 150m of each other. Several hearths within the causewayed enclosure and a series of fire settings along the infilled ditch of the cursus were the only clues to the activities that took place within them.

Neolithic polished flint axe found at Creech St Michael.

STONE TOOLS

Stone was still the main material used for making cutting tools, many of which were similar to their Mesolithic predecessors. The biggest technological change was the widespread use of polished flint, and other stone, axes. These tools would have been vital in the task of clearing the woodland for agriculture. Sometimes considerable effort was made to grind down the edges of the axes to produce a polished surface.

Some of the axes seem never to have been used but instead were kept as precious items signifying some special status or importance. When such precious items are found in perfect condition in pits, ditches or wetlands they were probably deposited as part of a ceremony, sometimes perhaps as an offering to a god or spirit.

TRADE AND EXCHANGE

Examination of the stone used to make axes has shown that many of the examples from Somerset had travelled great distances from where they were made in Cornwall, the Lake District and even the French Alps. Using similar techniques it has been discovered that pottery made in Cornwall was being used in Somerset and pots made near Frome were transported to Wiltshire. These artefacts would not have moved around by a process like modern trade. A more likely method would be as a formal exchange of gifts between two people or groups. The jadeite axe, from the Alps, found beside the Sweet Track was probably owned briefly by many different people before it ended up in a Somerset marsh.

WOODEN TRACKWAYS

In the wetlands of central Somerset Neolithic people made wooden trackways to allow them to cross the wet river valleys and to exploit the natural resources of those areas. Somerset has produced more examples of these prehistoric wooden trackways than the whole of the rest of England, Scotland and Wales put together.

One of these trackways, the Sweet Track, is also the oldest known wooden trackway in Great Britain, built

Reconstruction of the Sweet Track, built to cross 2km of reedswamp in 3806 BC. It was named after Ray Sweet, a local peat cutter who discovered it.

from wood felled in the winter of 3807/6 BC. It was built through a reed swamp over a distance of 2km between the Polden Hills and the (then) island of Westhay. It was made by resting a wooden rail on the peat surface under the water. Over this rail pairs of stakes were driven in at an angle to create a V-shaped cradle in which a split plank of oak or ash was laid to form a narrow walking platform above the water.

The only tools available to fell the trees, split the planks and cut the stakes would have been axes and knives of flint or stone, with wooden mallets and wedges. Just felling an

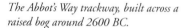

The Walton Heath trackway (built around 2800 BC) was made of thousands of coppiced hazel rods, woven into hurdles to provide a firm path across a raised bog.

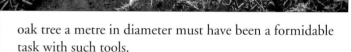

The Abbot's Way trackway, built across a raised bog around 2600 BC.

oak tree a metre in diameter must have been a formidable task with such tools.

Many other trackways were built later in the Neolithic across very wet woodland, raised bogs and tidal creeks. Brushwood tracks are the most common but there were also corduroy tracks (made of whole or half logs laid next to each other) such as the Abbot's Way, and paths made from woven hurdle panels like the Walton Heath track.

Examination of the wood from these trackways can show how people were using and altering the natural woodland. For instance, at the southern end of the Sweet Track small oak trees were used which grew after an area had been cleared of mature trees 100 years earlier. In contrast the lime and oak trees used to build the northern end were from a natural, dense, high-canopy woodland. Some of the oak trees from this woodland on Westhay island were over 400 years old and more than a metre in diameter when they were felled. Much of the material used in the hurdle trackways is from hazel trees that had been cut down and subsequently produced large numbers of long straight shoots from the stump. This technique, called coppicing, was later to become a very common form of woodland management, although in the Neolithic it may have been a less planned product of woodland clearance.

WOODEN TOOLS

Wooden artefacts do not normally survive from so long ago but the waterlogged peats of Somerset have produced important evidence for many wooden tools. All the axes would have needed handles and all the arrows would have had wooden shafts. One flint arrowhead from beside the Sweet Track retained traces of the hazel arrow shaft and the fine string made from nettle fibre that was used to bind them together. Fragments of Neolithic bows have also been found including a two-metre-long bow bound with leather that was found on Meare Heath. A replica of this bow has shown that it is capable of firing an arrow further than a medieval longbow.

A yew mallet and oak wedges found in the Brue valley would have been used in the splitting of trees into planks and the driving in of stakes. A wooden stirrer was discovered beside the Sweet Track in a broken pot containing hazel nuts. Other everyday items included yew pins, whittled to a point at one end and carefully polished. They may have been used to hold clothes or hair in place or as bag fasteners. A piece of rolled-up bark from Ashcott Heath may have been used as a Neolithic bead, and a small wooden tomahawk from the Sweet Track was probably a child's toy.

Stuart Prior fires a replica of the Meare Heath bow.

Neolithic bowl and wooden stirrer found beside the Sweet Track.

31

THE BRONZE AGE

INTRODUCTION

The use of tools made of copper, and later of bronze, first occurred shortly before 2000 BC. This introduction of metalwork was soon followed by a new ceramic style known as Beaker pottery after the distinctive shape of the vessels. Between 2000 BC and *c.* 600 BC our interpretation of prehistoric society is dominated by the changes in the styles and technology of pottery production and metalworking. We know that major changes were also occurring in the landscape but there has been little research on the settlements and field systems of this period in Somerset.

SETTLEMENTS

Only four Bronze Age settlements have been subjected to large-scale archaeological excavation. One lay on the southern side of Brean Down where four phases of Bronze Age occupation were separated by layers of blown sand and hillwash material. Two of the phases produced evidence of buildings, the earliest being an oval stone-walled hut, and, from the later period, two circular huts terraced into the hillside with walls partly of stone and partly of timber. The bone remains show us that the domesticated animals of these farmers were mainly cattle, sheep and pigs in addition to a small number of dogs, horses and a cat. Wild food included deer, shellfish, birds and fish, and salt was made by evaporating seawater. The last vestiges of another Bronze Age roundhouse were excavated in advance of a housing development at Nerrol's Farm, near Taunton, and the third site was at Podimore, near Yeovilton, where two roundhouses were excavated. The other site was Sigwells, near South Cadbury, where a rectangular enclosure contained a roundhouse and almost 400 fragments of moulds for casting bronze.

On Exmoor the remains of many roundhouses exist as low earth banks or stone walls. Some of these probably date to the Bronze Age but none has been excavated, and it is possible that they could be of the Iron Age. Other evidence for possible settlement sites comes from the finds of pottery and flint of the period, as at Cannard's Grave near Shepton Mallet, Vinny Combe in West Quantoxhead and several of the small sand 'islands' on the northern edge of the Polden Hills. Ditches at Southay and Poundisford Park, and pits at Lower Wilton Farm (Curry Rivel), Dimmer and Odcombe are all probably part of Bronze Age settlements, but no evidence for the actual houses has been found.

Bronze Age flint and pottery has also been found in Cheddar Gorge in caves such as Chelm's Combe, Soldier's Hole, Sun Hole and Gough's Cave, but there is nothing to suggest that they were occupied for any length of time. Elsewhere the sites of the Iron Age hillforts at Ham Hill and South Cadbury have all produced Bronze Age finds, while at Norton Camp (Norton Fitzwarren), a Middle Bronze Age enclosure, defined by a bank and ditch, was found during excavations, from which a hoard of eight bracelets and three axes was recovered.

THE LANDSCAPE DIVIDED UP

It is in the Bronze Age that the first evidence exists for major physical division of the landscape in Britain. In Somerset this is most readily apparent on Exmoor where the traces of the prehistoric landscape have not been masked or destroyed by later activity. By studying earthworks and air photographs a large area of prehistoric fields has been detected, consisting of small square or rectangular fields defined by low stone banks, or by lynchets where they run across the slope. These field systems are present on Codsend and Hoar Moors, Almsworthy Common, Withycombe Hill, Little Tom's Hill, Great Hill and Honeycombe Hill (Luccombe). They are often associated with small settlements consisting of four or five stone-walled roundhouses, sometimes all contained within an enclosure.

None of these fields or settlements has been excavated, so it is not known exactly when they were laid out. From Codsend and Hoar Moors pollen evidence has shown, however, that significant clearance of the local woodland for agriculture began in the Middle Bronze Age. This, together with evidence for large-scale Bronze Age land division in Dartmoor and Wiltshire, suggests that the fields and

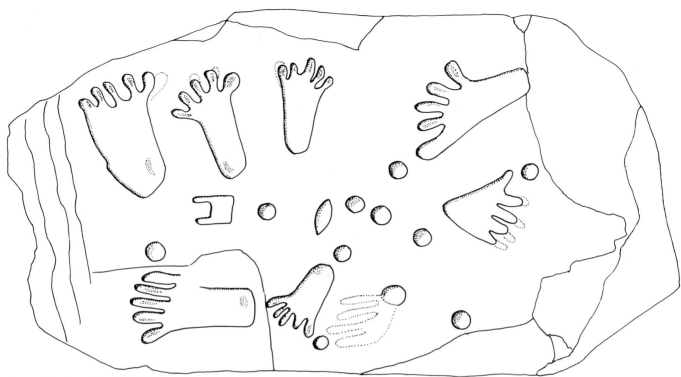

Cup marks and carvings of feet found on the inner face of one of the slabs of a stone cist that lay beneath a round barrow at Pool Farm, Priddy. The cist contained a cremation burial dating to c. 1840 BC. The slab is 1.3m in length.

settlements on Exmoor also originated at this time.

Away from Exmoor, the evidence for land division is limited. The most extensive evidence comes from Sigwells, near South Cadbury, where geophysical survey has revealed an extensive field system shown by excavation to date to the Early Bronze Age. There is also an earth bank on Brean Down and examples of existing field boundaries at Shapwick and Hillfarrance were found to follow the line of Bronze Age banks and ditches. A much larger feature, Dead Woman's Ditch, which extends for over a kilometre across the Quantock Hills, is probably of this date. Even the wetlands of central Somerset may have witnessed the construction of some physical boundaries, as at Harter's Hill on Queen's Sedgemoor where two or three rows of large oak piles have been traced from the edge of the hill for 100m into the prehistoric wetland with no sign of stopping.

STONE SETTINGS

Many standing stones have been found in Somerset, the vast majority on Exmoor. There is little evidence for when these stones were erected but some of the stone rows are aligned on Bronze Age barrows, which suggests that they may be of the same date. Over thirty single or double standing stones are known, mostly fairly small but some quite large like the Whit Stones at Porlock, which stand 1.5m high. They may have served a function as significant marker points in the landscape, and many of them have performed this role up to the present day. They may also be the focal points for ritual activities such as burial, but no significant excavation of the land around these features has taken place to test this possibility.

A dozen stone rows have been identified on Exmoor. Some of these may have performed an important role in dividing up the landscape as they extend for a considerable distance. At Culbone Hill, Oare, for example, twenty-one stones are set over 371m and twelve stones at Madacombe cover 286m. Other shorter rows sometimes lead up to barrows, as at Kittuck and Porlock Allotment. The functions of many of the rows are harder to suggest as, for example, the fourteen stones at Almsworthy, which form four short rows or the three rows of three stones at Beckham Hill.

Some groups of stones were obviously defining a special area important to the social or ritual life of the community. The most obvious of these are the three stone circles on Exmoor at Porlock Allotment, Withypool Hill, and Hoaroak Hill. Elsewhere on the moor the square or quadrilateral groupings at Squallacombe, Trout Hill and Westermill, and the V-shaped stone group at Ricksey Ball, may have had a similar function.

Two Somerset stones have some decoration. A recumbent stone at Hythe, Cheddar, was probably once a standing stone as it is decorated with cup marks on both sides. A barrow at Pool Farm, Priddy, which was destroyed for road widening in 1931, had a stone-lined chamber, and one of these slabs was found to have decorative impressions of feet, cup marks and a horned device.

Barrows

Barrows are the most common form of monument that we know of from the Bronze Age, not least because they are often prominent features in the landscape and are therefore easy to detect. There are as many as 550 barrows in Somerset, although the exact number is uncertain because they can sometimes be confused with other earthworks such as clearance cairns, peat burning mounds, windmill mounds and spoil heaps from mining activity.

Barrows are mainly concentrated on Mendip, Exmoor and the Quantock Hills, with a small group on the Blackdown Hills. Many of these barrows were deliberately situated at the tops of slopes where they could be seen from a wide area. They sometimes occur singly, or in groups of two or three, but barrow cemeteries are also common, having up to as many as sixteen barrows in one group as at Beacon Hill, Doulting. The barrows in these cemeteries

either occur in lines, as at Priddy Nine Barrows and West Cranmore, or in more irregular clusters as at Pen Hill Wood and Slab House Inn, St Cuthbert Out, Wells, and Stock Hill, Chewton Mendip.

Many barrows were 'opened' in the 18th and 19th centuries by antiquarians or treasure hunters. Often the only surviving evidence of this activity is a dip left by the digging in the centre of the barrow, or in some cases a brief description of what was found. There have been very few well-recorded, scientific excavations of barrows in Somerset to counterbalance this loss of information, and there have been no excavations at all in the last thirty years, apart from at Carscliff where only the edge of the barrow was excavated.

The internal structures of barrows vary enormously. The earthwork that covers the burial can be composed wholly of earth or of stones, or a combination of the two. Stone barrows, or cairns, may simply use surface material but often ditches are dug around the barrows to supply material for the mound and sometimes also an outer bank. Barrows with a closely-set central mound, ditch and outer bank are often called saucer barrows, while if they have a flat area (a berm) between the mound and the ditch they are termed bell barrows. Turf, stripped from a large surrounding area, was also often used to form the mound material. Kerbs of large stones were sometimes placed to help retain the material of both stone and earthen mounds, and also no doubt helped to enhance the visual effect.

Unlike Neolithic long barrows, round barrows do not contain the bones of numerous people all mixed together. Usually the barrow was initially built over the remains of a single individual, often placed in a pit or stone-lined cist. This was a burial rite that developed at the very end of the Neolithic period and continued until the Late Bronze Age. There is often evidence for the later, or secondary, burial of the remains of other individuals higher up in the mound or nearer the edge. At Tynings Farm, Cheddar, the barrow was increased in height and width when a secondary cremation burial was added and the surrounding ditch was re-cut with the causeway across it moved to a new place.

Barrows that date from the Beaker period usually

The Ashen Hill linear barrow cemetery with the Priddy Nine Barrows in the background.

contain inhumations as opposed to the cremation burials that became usual by the Middle Bronze Age. Beaker burials are usually in a crouched position, often accompanied by the distinctive Beaker pottery and sometimes flint tools, as at Culbone Hill, Oare, or Wick Barrow, Stogursey. Some Beaker graves do not appear to been marked by mounds, as for example at Greylake sand quarry, Barwick quarry, Windmill Hill quarry (Wincanton) and the one in the ditch of Gorsey Bigbury henge.

Cremation burials have been found in over two thirds of the excavated barrows. At the Sigwells III barrow in Charlton Horethorne a large amount of charcoal and some post holes suggest that the cremation took place where the mound was subsequently built. Sometimes the cremated material was placed directly on a stone slab, but more often it was contained within a special burial urn, often turned upside down, sometimes on a slab. As well as urns the cremations are sometimes accompanied by small 'pygmy

Beakers excavated from Wick Barrow, Stogursey, in 1907. Each beaker accompanied a burial that lay in a crouched position.

cups', bronze daggers and beads of amber, jet or faience (a type of glass) as at Tynings Farm, Cheddar. Flint artefacts such as scrapers or saws are common, while more unusual finds include bronze razors, awls, horse skulls and the hoard of ten to twenty bronze artefacts from Westbury Beacon barrow that were recorded in 1816 as having been sold for two gallons of cider.

Not all the people of the Bronze Age were buried in barrows. At Mendip Lodge Wood in Priddy there were 70 to 80 pits, many of which contained cremations, urns and bronze daggers. These burials, like the Beaker burials found in quarries, may represent a more numerous but less easily detected method of disposing of the dead. Very little evidence exists in Somerset or elsewhere in England for the disposal of the dead in the Late Bronze Age and Early Iron Age. A poorly-recorded burial at Hendford Hill, Yeovil, is practically the only example from Somerset.

Outside Somerset there is some evidence of human bones, but rarely whole skeletons, from the pits and ditches of settlements and from rivers or other wet places. The peat of the Somerset moors is normally so acidic it destroys bone material, but at Greylake on Sedgemoor it is less acidic and human bones from the Late Bronze Age have been found accompanied by sheep jaw-bones, pottery and a bronze axe in what was then an area of shallow water surrounded by sedges and reeds. The site was marked out by oak posts that projected above the water. The body, or bodies, had probably been defleshed by excarnation (exposure) before being deposited in the water.

The wetlands

The broad valleys of central Somerset were a vast area of wetland during the Bronze Age and the analysis of plant and beetle remains preserved in the peat has allowed us to reconstruct the landscape in this area. The Brue valley, where most of the archaeological investigation has taken place, was dominated by a raised bog formed from sphagnum moss, cotton grass and heather. At the eastern end of the valley, and to the south of the Polden Hills on Sedgemoor, the environment was more diverse with wet fen woodland, reed beds and areas of open water surrounded by sedges in addition to the raised bog.

This wetland environment would have been an important source of food in the form of fish, wildfowl and mammals, and would have provided reed for thatching, wood for making baskets and otter and beaver pelts for winter clothing. To enter and cross the raised bogs it was frequently necessary to build wooden trackways. Over nineteen groups of Bronze Age trackways have been found in Somerset. Some of them are very short, designed to provide sure footing over particularly wet parts of the bog surface. Others are several kilometres in length and run from the Polden ridge across the bog to, and between, the (then) islands of Meare, Westhay and Burtle.

The most common way of making a trackway was simply to dump armfuls of brushwood down on the bog surface and peg them in place at the sides. The Tinney's Ground tracks are made in this way and represent many phases of trackway construction over a long period always going in the same direction. For other routes, such as the Eclipse track, narrow hazel stems were selected to make large hurdle panels which were then laid flat on the bog surface. The most complex structure was the Meare Heath trackway. In the wettest areas the track was built on a layer of brushwood. On top of this, wooden beams were laid across the line of the track like railway sleepers, and were staked in place through holes at the end

of the beams. Split planks were then laid on top of the 'sleepers' to form the walking platform.

Very little is known about the settlements of the trackway builders, but something is known of the dryland landscape that surrounded the wetlands because of the pollen that was blown into the bogs and preserved in the peat. This information shows us that the woodland cover was steadily decreasing during the Bronze Age as larger areas were cleared for agriculture. There were, however, some short periods when woodland cover was re-established in some places and in the Late Bronze Age (around 1100 BC) the changing bog vegetation suggests that the climate was getting wetter, which may have made arable farming more difficult.

The Eclipse Track, built around 1800 BC, used 2m long hurdles of woven hazel rods to cross over 1km of raised bog.

METALWORK

Large numbers of bronze tools have been found in Somerset. Daggers and knives sometimes accompanied the dead in barrows but in other places the metalwork is dominated by different types of axes, with spearheads and swords becoming more common in the later Bronze Age. Many pieces of metalwork have been found singly but hoards of material are also known. Some of these, such as the Wick Park hoard from Stogursey, were so-called founder's hoards composed of many different types of broken bronze objects collected together for melting down and recasting.

Most of the metalwork was not collected for such utilitarian purposes but appears to have been deliberately placed, possibly

Bronze Age hoard comprising sickles, palstaves, bracelets and rings found in peat near Edington Burtle in 1854. The bronzes, which date to 1400–1200 BC, were found in a small wooden box that disintegrated shortly after discovery.

One half of a Middle Bronze Age bronze mould for casting a particularly large socketed spearhead 295mm in length. It was found at East Pennard.

as a ritual offering. Much of the isolated metalwork has been found in river valleys and can be seen as part of a water-associated cult that became increasingly important towards the later Bronze Age. Many very valuable artefacts such as the two Late Bronze Age swords at Pitney, or the palstave axe complete with its shaft from King's Sedgemoor, were undoubtedly deposited in very wet environments. The large Middle Bronze Age hoard discovered during peat digging at Edington must also have been placed in a wet environment as it was contained in a wooden box. It is only at Greylake (see above) that a structure has been found with such metalwork, but this may be because the bronze objects from the river valleys are almost always chance finds rather than from excavations.

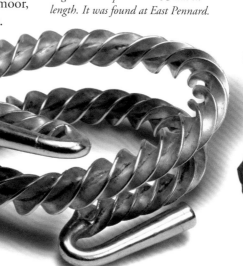

Middle Bronze Age gold torc found on Hendford Hill, Yeovil. It is one of only a small number of Bronze Age gold objects found in the county.

All the changes of metalworking design can be seen in the Somerset evidence. Early designs are represented by such finds as the three flanged axes discovered during construction of the Milverton bypass. It is in the Middle Bronze Age that the Somerset metalworking tradition really begins to thrive to the extent that the main metalworking tradition in England at this time is called the Taunton phase. It is represented by numerous hoards at places including Edington, Weare, Spaxton, Wedmore, Badgworth, Norton Fitzwarren, Bishops Lydeard and Taunton Workhouse. This phase has also been called the Ornament Horizon because of the large numbers of metal personal ornaments found in the hoards including twisted torcs (neck rings), arm rings, bracelets, finger rings and quoit-head pins.

Late Bronze Age metalwork is less common but the Somerset industry is important enough to have another metalworking tradition named after Stogursey where a large founder's hoard was discovered in 1870. It consisted of 20 sword fragments, 29 socketed axes, 37 fragments of socketed axes, two palstaves, two gouges, two daggers, a chape (part of a sword scabbard), 20 complete or fragmentary spearheads and 34 bronze fragments.

Sheet bronze shield dating to 1200–1000 BC found during excavations at South Cadbury. The metal is less than 1mm in thickness making the shield an object of status or display rather than a means of defence. It had been placed front down in the corner of a ditch and stabbed three times, perhaps representing its ritual 'killing'. The shield is 665mm in diameter.

The Iron Age

Early Iron Age

The Iron Age traditionally covers the period from 700 BC to AD 43. The beginning of this period, when iron was replacing bronze as the primary raw material for making tools and weapons, is at present poorly understood in Somerset. It is clear, however, that life continued much as in the later Bronze Age. Distinctive pottery of the period has been found at a number of sites in the south-east of the county including Ham Hill and Cadbury Castle. A small open agricultural settlement, with post-built structures, a possible round house and associated pits, has been revealed at the latter site.

Hillforts

Hillforts are the largest and most dramatic prehistoric monuments in Somerset. They range in size from less than one hectare up to 88 hectares, no doubt reflecting varied political and social organisation. Most appear today as grassy banks and ditches with entrances consisting of a simple gap in the ramparts or passageways created by an inward or outward turn in the ramparts. Their eroded and silted condition gives a diminished impression of their original appearance. Few hillforts have been excavated, but where this has happened a complex sequence of construction, repair and renewal has been revealed.

In the 6th and 5th centuries BC many communities in

Harold St George Gray's excavation across the ditch at Norton Fitzwarren hillfort in 1908. Roman pottery was found in the upper 1.5m of silt, with Iron Age material below that and Bronze Age sherds at the base of the 2.75m deep ditch.

Aerial view of Cadbury Castle with the village of South Cadbury in the background. The ramparts which surround the hilltop are mostly covered by trees but are visible towards the right.

Somerset (and southern Britain in general) felt compelled to construct these defences, probably as a result of a greater importance being placed on land ownership and territories than in preceding periods. Some hillforts, such as Brent Knoll and Cow Castle, were located in highly defensible positions on the tops of steep-sided hills, but others were more easily approached, such as Maesbury. Early hillforts were defended by a single bank and ditch following the contour of a hill and with one or perhaps two entrances. In the 4th to 3rd centuries BC many hillforts appear to have gone out of regular use but those that continued to be occupied often underwent modifications including the addition of further ramparts and ditches.

Cadbury Castle is the most extensively investigated hillfort in the county as the result of excavations carried out there between 1966 and 1973. The view from the hilltop, particularly to the north, is impressive and includes Glastonbury Tor and the Glamorgan Hills in the distance. The first phase of defence consisted of a single bank and ditch enclosing an area of 7.5 hectares. The rampart consisted of an open timber framework filled with earth and limestone rubble derived from the outer ditch. Horizontal wooden planks, later replaced by dry-stone walling, gave the rampart a vertical external facing. In the 4th century BC the site was further strengthened by the construction of between two and three additional ramparts down-slope of

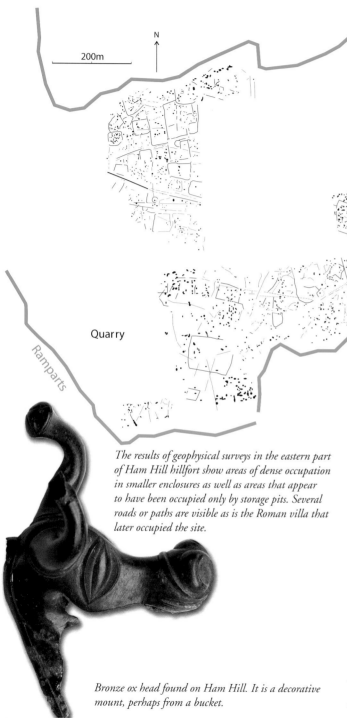

N

200m

Villa

Quarry

Ramparts

The results of geophysical surveys in the eastern part of Ham Hill hillfort show areas of dense occupation in smaller enclosures as well as areas that appear to have been occupied only by storage pits. Several roads or paths are visible as is the Roman villa that later occupied the site.

Bronze ox head found on Ham Hill. It is a decorative mount, perhaps from a bucket.

the original defences. Gaps on the south-west, north-east and east sides all represent original entrances. The south-west gateway has been excavated and here, over the centuries, the passage of feet, hooves and wheels wore away the living rock creating a hollow-way two metres deep. Guard chambers were constructed in the ends of the inner ramparts and there were substantial gates protecting the entranceway. By the 4th century BC a substantial residential population living in round houses occupied Cadbury Castle. Many of the houses appear to have been repaired or rebuilt on a number of occasions, sometimes on the same spot, sometimes in a slightly different position. Contemporary with these houses were large numbers of storage pits.

By far the largest hillfort in the county (if not the country) is Ham Hill. The main body of the hillfort is sub-rectangular in shape and is surrounded by a single bank and ditch with a smaller outer bank, enclosing an area of 88 hectares. A fan-shaped extension to the north is more strongly defended with two ramparts, two ditches and an outer bank. In spite of its size there were probably only two entrances.

Finds from the northern spur on Ham Hill, largely retrieved during quarrying in the mid-19th to early 20th centuries, indicate that this area was the major focus of activity in the later Bronze Age, Iron Age and early Roman periods. In the 1990s the Royal Commission on the Historical Monuments of England commissioned an extensive programme of geophysical survey on the unquarried areas of Ham Hill. The results of the survey, combined with data derived from air photographs, revealed a complex arrangement of enclosures, roadways, pits and roundhouses.

Hillforts were enormous undertakings. The circuits of the Cadbury Castle and Ham Hill defences, for example, run for over one kilometre and five kilometres respectively. They would have involved a large number of people in their construction, certainly more than those occupying the sites.

The additional labour perhaps came from the surrounding population in the quieter periods of the farming cycle. Once completed, maintenance of the defences would have required a significant and on-going commitment of labour. Hillforts clearly served a defensive function, but display and symbol were also important motivating factors. Designed to exclude people, they also served to impress. They are seen as focal points for the surrounding communities.

Traditionally hillforts have been regarded as the residences of kings or chiefs but opinion is shifting to the view that occupation was more communal and egalitarian. Whilst hillforts produce weaponry including swords, daggers, spearheads and quantities of clay and stone sling shot, finds overwhelmingly relate to domestic, farming, craft and industrial activities. Raw materials and finished products show the hillforts to have been part of a complex network of trade and exchange. Cadbury Castle has produced decorated pottery from Mendip, Devon and Cornwall, shale from Dorset, amber from the Baltic, whetstones from near Plymouth and quern stones from Pen Pits (15km to the north-east), Beacon Hill (21km to the north) and other Mendip sources.

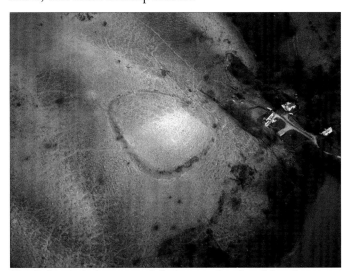

Trendle Ring is the best preserved of a large number of small Iron Age enclosures built on the slopes (rather than the tops) of the Quantock Hills and elsewhere in the county.

West Somerset has few classic hillforts. Most are relatively small and, like Bats Castle, sited around the edge of Exmoor. The area has rather more examples of monuments known as hill-slope enclosures. Small in area, they predominantly occur, as their name implies, on the sides of hills. Trendle Ring, for example, is situated on a steeply-sloping spur on the west side of the Quantock Hills. Hillsides are less easily defensible positions and these sites presumably served different purposes from those on hilltops. Little archaeological work has been carried out on hill-slope enclosures, making their date of construction, internal arrangements and functions uncertain. Some were perhaps settlement sites. Others may have been for the pounding of stock. Usage of these sites seems to have spanned the later Bronze Age to Roman periods, perhaps even later.

OTHER SETTLEMENTS

Whilst warfare and the threat of conflict were factors in the Iron Age, it is becoming clear that southern Britain was overwhelmingly a land of farmers. Wherever the environment could support it, the landscape was one of arable, pasture and managed woodland, dotted with farmsteads and field systems. With few exceptions, relatively little is known about non-hillfort settlements in Somerset, although there were undoubtedly substantial numbers of them. Some were surrounded by an enclosing bank and ditch but others were not enclosed. Large numbers of enclosed settlements are known from aerial photography on the lower slopes of the Quantock Hills but the unenclosed sites are much harder to identify. One small settlement or farmstead that lay within an open environment, probably of grassland, was excavated in advance of road building at Canard's Grave, Shepton Mallet, in 1995. The sites of four round houses dating to the period 500 to 300 BC were identified. Finds of pottery and other artefacts on a number of Roman sites in the south-east of the county, in particular villas, indicate that some, perhaps many, of these sites were first occupied in the Iron Age.

The 'lake villages' of Glastonbury and Meare are the

most extensively excavated and best-preserved Iron Age sites in Somerset, although their location and preservation of finds make them untypical. Glastonbury lake village was constructed on an artificial island of timber, stone and clay located in an environment of open water, reeds and fenwood, probably best described as a swamp. The island served as the foundation for an ever-changing settlement. In its early stages the site comprised five or six houses, one of which burnt down, and a series of clay spreads which provided bases for outdoor work. As the number of occupants grew, the island was extended and more houses were built. Everything required to sustain life in this permanently-occupied settlement had to be ferried in by log boat or raft.

At its greatest extent, Glastonbury lake village comprised perhaps fifteen houses and had a population of 200 people.

The houses were circular, with walls of vertical posts in-filled with wattle and daub. Roofs were thatched with reed or straw. Many of the clay floors supported hearths, some for cooking and warmth, others for industrial purposes. An irregular palisade of stout posts ran around the edge of the site. It was probably designed to prevent the island spreading and sinking rather than for defence. On the eastern side of the settlement there was a landing stage constructed of clay, rubble and wood for water traffic. Ultimately rising water levels made continued occupation of the island impossible and the inhabitants were forced to leave. Permanently water-logged ever since, enormous quantities of timber were preserved and exposed during excavations between 1892 and 1907.

At Meare there were two areas of occupation known as Meare Village West and Meare Village East. The

Reconstruction view of Glastonbury Lake Village by Amédée Forestier, published in the Illustrated London News *in 1911. Recent work has shown that the buildings were fewer in number and less densely spaced.*

Oak log boat found in peat at Shapwick in 1906. Six metres in length, it is one of many that would have been used to transport people, animals and goods across the wetlands of the Somerset Levels in the Iron Age.

structure and environment of the Meare sites differed from Glastonbury lake village. They lay on two small humps of raised bog about 60m apart, separated by a very wet reed swamp and just a short distance to the north of the island that now holds the villages of Meare and Westhay. There was a large pool of water or a very wet marsh immediately north of the sites. Although some timber was used to create a firm foundation for occupation, and clay was imported for use as floors, the location was significantly drier than that of Glastonbury lake village. There is little evidence for substantial buildings at Meare. Circles and arcs of stakes are thought to represent temporary shelters, perhaps tents. Meare was probably occupied seasonally or periodically between periods of flooding.

Reconstruction of a Glastonbury Lake Village round house at the Peat Moors Centre, Westhay.

Glass beads and antler combs, some of the rich evidence for domestic life and craft activity at Meare Lake Village. The yellow decorated bead was made at Meare, the combs were used in the production of woollen braids.

Glastonbury lake village and the Meare sites provide similar and unparalleled evidence for the lives of their occupants. On the personal side are beads, brooches, finger rings, armlets, toggles and tweezers. Bone dice indicate that games were played. There is abundant evidence for diet. Most food derived from farming the nearby dry land but wild animals, such as boar and deer, were hunted and wild plants, nuts and berries were collected. Unusually for the Iron Age, but perhaps not surprising in a location such as this, fish were also eaten. Craft and industrial activities included bone and antler working, bronze casting, iron smithing, shale working, wood working, spinning and weaving. An exceptional number of weaving combs at Meare show braid production to have been an important activity. Meare is also one of the few sites in Europe with evidence for glass working. Small yellow annular beads and globular beads of clear glass inlaid with yellow spirals or chevrons were made on-site and afterwards travelled near and far. Some eventually reached the north of Scotland. In spite of their seemingly isolated and marginal positions these sites were certainly not backwaters.

Activity at Meare began in *c.* 300 BC, while Glastonbury lake village was established about one hundred years later. Occupation at both sites ended in about 50 BC. The relationship between the sites, which lay just 5km apart, is unclear.

Several cave sites were also occupied in this period. Wookey Hole is of particular importance and finds suggest that activity there was contemporary with the lake villages.

An enclosure identified at Ilchester appears to represent the establishment of a new form of site in the region towards the end of the Iron Age. Some 16 hectares in area and surrounded by a substantial bank and ditch, it was situated in the bottom of the valley of the River Yeo, a location which was probably only suitable for seasonal use. As yet, little is known about the internal arrangement of the site but it may bear comparison with *oppida*, enclosures being established in south-eastern England at this time as tribal centres of political, economic and religious importance.

TERRITORIES

Monuments and finds such as pottery and coins enable regional groupings to be defined. Somerset lay at the convergence of three tribal areas in the Late Iron Age, namely the territories of the Durotriges, Dobunni and Dumnonii. The Durotriges were centred upon Dorset and south-east Somerset, the Dobunni covered Gloucestershire and north-east Somerset and the Dumnonii extended from west Somerset through Devon and Cornwall.

Boundaries between tribal areas probably shifted over time and are therefore difficult to define with precision. Evidence from elsewhere suggests that tribal boundaries were not a thin line but a fairly broad swathe, perhaps up to 30km wide, and often focused upon major rivers or wetlands. The boundary between the Dumnonii and the Durotriges probably lay along the line of the rivers Parrett and Axe. Glastonbury lake village and the Meare settlements may have lain within a watery no-man's land between the Dobunni and Durotriges and served as important points of contact for purposes such as trade, gift exchange and communication.

Gold coin struck in the name of Eisu of the Dobunni tribe. It was discovered at Stogursey, some distance to the west of the tribal territory.

RITUAL AND BURIAL

In recent years it has become apparent that spiritual and ritual activity was integrated into daily life and was not necessarily confined to special places. Material once interpreted as discarded rubbish is now seen in a different way, as part of a process of ritual deposition. Quern stones, iron torcs (neck rings) and iron 'currency bars' have been found in pits on Ham Hill where another pit, discovered in the 19th century, is said to have contained 15 human skulls. Horse and ox skulls and occasionally complete pots were carefully placed in pits at Cadbury Castle. Here, also, there was a group of over thirty newborn calf burials dating to near the end of the Iron Age. Slightly later, a small rectangular timber building interpreted as a porched shrine was constructed close by the calf burials. Votive deposits associated with hillfort defences have been found at Kingsdown Camp, Mells, and Cadbury Castle, while four complete adult human skulls – three male and one female and bearing sword cuts – were found in close proximity to the timber palisade surrounding Glastonbury lake village. A fine bronze sword scabbard discovered in the peat at Meare Heath might also be a votive offering.

Evidence for the treatment of the dead is very limited as they seem usually to have been disposed of in a way that left little or no archaeological trace. There are a few exceptions. A Late Iron-Age dagger, with its sheath and associated belt fittings, and an iron adze were found with a cremation burial in a pit on Ham Hill. Glastonbury lake village produced some evidence for burial. A number of neonatal burials were found, usually placed on or below clay floors. The charred remains of an adult were found outside the palisade. Animal bones including cow, pig, sheep/goat and possibly frog accompanied this burial and are perhaps evidence for associated rites. Records exist of human skeletons having been discovered at a number of hillforts, for example King's Castle, Wiveliscombe, where human remains were found during quarrying in the early 19th century. Details and dating evidence are lacking and the remains may be associated with the Roman invasion.

Dagger and sheath discovered with an Iron Age cremation burial on Ham Hill.

The Roman Period

Introduction

Somerset became part of the Roman empire shortly after the invasion of AD 43. The two tribes inhabiting the area, the Durotriges in the south and the Dumnonii in the west, seem to have been hostile to the idea judging from the historical sources and from the presence of early Roman military equipment at hillforts such as South Cadbury and Ham Hill.

Sheet bronze face plaque found in debris in a guard chamber at the south-west gate of Cadbury Castle. The guard chamber was destroyed in the mid-1st century AD. The plaque was probably a decorative mount for a piece of furniture.

The picture from the excavations at South Cadbury is, however, more complicated. Following the destruction of the south-west gate by fire there seems to have been a period of abandonment before the roadway was resurfaced and a major rebuilding began. Beneath the roadway were found the scattered remains of at least 22 people ranging from about 4 to 35 years of age with nearly one third children. Some of the bones bore evidence of violence, including part of a sword-slashed skull, and many had been burnt. Initially interpreted as a 'massacre' of the inhabitants by the Romans, it now seems that the bones had been brought from elsewhere and buried as part of the refurbishment of the gateway. This suggests, as does the rebuilding,

that occupation continued following a Roman attack. The new gateway was also destroyed by fire and this may be associated with the construction of Roman military buildings on the hilltop. The dating of these two events is not certain but the refurbishment of the gateway must have happened well after the initial conquest and radiocarbon dates show continuing activity into the 2nd century.

On Ham Hill, finds of armour and armour fittings and spear and ballista bolt heads (from a large Roman catapult), mainly on the northern spur, provide clear evidence for a Roman military presence in the mid-1st century AD. Both infantry and cavalry units were present. These objects plus contemporary brooches and pottery probably indicate some form of temporary military base on the hilltop.

It is likely that forts were eventually established at both South Cadbury and Ham Hill, but the evidence suggests that, rather than happening following the conquest, this may have been related to disturbances in the later 1st century such as those following the Boudiccan revolt in AD 60–61.

The location of forts suggests that some were sited to guard the supply route of the Fosse Way. One is certainly known at Ilchester, controlling the site of the Late Iron Age 'oppidum' and the river crossing, and the spacing of known forts suggests that another was located at Shepton Mallet, and perhaps another near Cricket St Thomas.

Away from the Fosse Way, other forts were established around Exmoor (at Wiveliscombe, Upton and in Devon), and at Charterhouse, which oversaw the lead mining. The discovery of the fort at Upton as recently as the 1990s suggests that more remain to be found.

Section of scale armour found on Ham Hill dating from shortly after the Roman invasion of Britain in AD 43.

Roman policy was to assimilate pre-existing social structures into the empire, a policy that gave local leaders a vested interest in conforming. This seems to have led to the rapid incorporation of the area into the civil organisation of the empire with the Second Legion leaving Exeter in the 70s and most forts being abandoned at a similar date. Civilian government was organised on the basis of self-governing city states modelled on those in the Mediterranean. The Civitas Durotrigium and Civitas Dumnoniorum were established, with towns at Dorchester and Exeter. The local aristocracy became members of the council but for most of the population life is likely to have continued much as before.

Towns

It is likely that civilian settlement at Ilchester grew around the fort and then spread to cover the area when the army left. Little is known of Ilchester in the early Roman period because of the destructive effects of later settlement, but the last two centuries of the Roman period saw the construction of imposing stone houses, many provided with mosaic floors. Also in the later period the town was enclosed by an earthen bank which later had a stone wall added to the front. Whilst the defensive function of these might seem obvious, it is clear from Ilchester and other towns that prestige played a large part in their construction. At Ilchester this is suggested by the fact that the south gate (at least) was constructed in stone at the same time as, or slightly before, the earth bank to provide an impressive entrance. The presence of walls, wealthy houses, and the dense cluster of villas around the town suggest that Ilchester was of some importance in later Roman Britain and inscriptions from Hadrian's Wall may imply that the Civitas Durotrigium was divided into two with Ilchester becoming the capital of the northern part.

Ilchester contrasts with the situation at Shepton Mallet

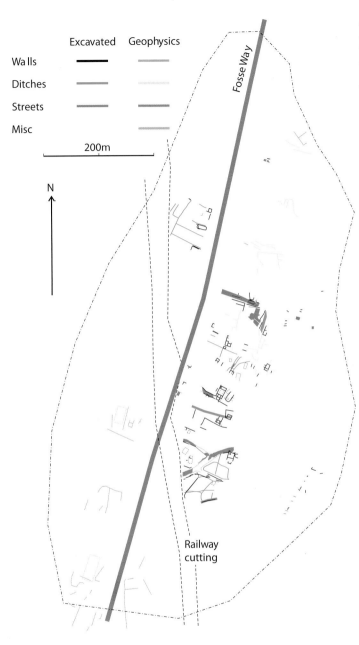

Plan of the features recorded at the Roman town of Shepton Mallet. The town lies astride the Fosse Way and has seen extensive excavations in advance of the construction of a business park. Unlike Ilchester it was not walled and no public buildings have been found.

where a small Roman town has been discovered over the last 15 years. While no evidence of a fort has been found it is likely that one was established during the 1st century, perhaps associated with an early pottery kiln found in the 19th century. The town grew up along both sides of the Fosse Way with roads and enclosures containing buildings.

Although some of the later buildings were of substantial stone construction there is no evidence of mosaics or any other indications of great wealth or status. In the later period some of the enclosures were used for burial, which suggests that Shepton Mallet was not legally a town – where burial would have been prohibited. At Ilchester substantial cemeteries have been discovered outside the walls, lying along the roads outside the town.

Some other settlements may have grown large enough for us to consider them towns. These include Cheddar, Westland at Yeovil (if these two are not large villas), the mining settlement at Charterhouse, and the ports at Combwich and Crandon Bridge.

THE COUNTRYSIDE

In the countryside the initial impact of Rome is hardly visible. Most of the enclosed and unenclosed prehistoric settlements that have been excavated show evidence of continued occupation. The finds show easier access to luxury goods such as fine pottery and metalwork but otherwise little change.

One new class of rural site does emerge: the villa. The Romanised aristocracy needed to impress the general population and other aristocrats in a society that was no longer allowed to be war-like with status based on heroism in battle. The answer seems to have been the villa, an impressive country residence close to the town where civic duties needed to be performed. Villas vary enormously in their size and elaboration but all are testimony to the wealth that the elite could acquire. Even the simplest show features that indicate the aspirations of the inhabitants. They are based on classical ideas of architecture, being rectangular and symmetrical, and often approached across a courtyard. They also aspired to bath houses, mosaics and underfloor

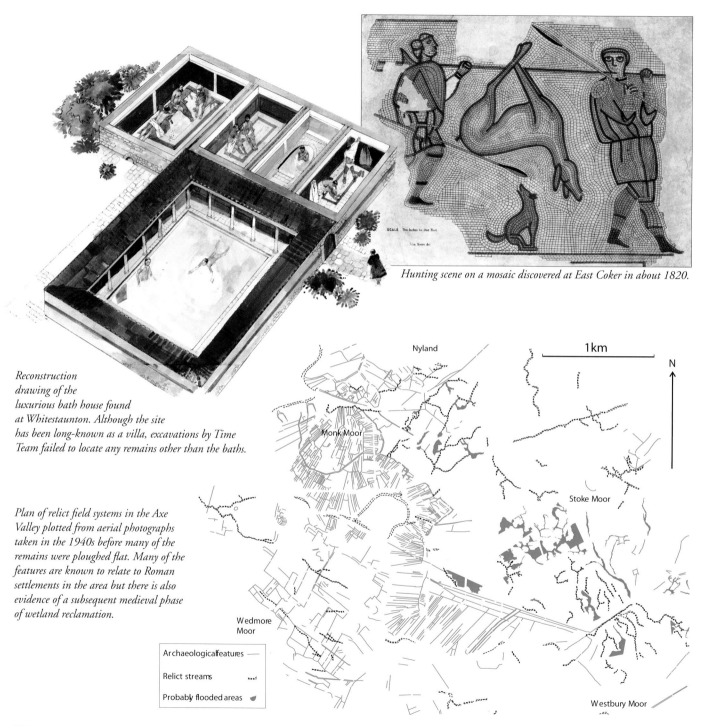

Hunting scene on a mosaic discovered at East Coker in about 1820.

SCALE Two Inches to One Foot

Reconstruction drawing of the luxurious bath house found at Whitestaunton. Although the site has been long-known as a villa, excavations by Time Team failed to locate any remains other than the baths.

Plan of relict field systems in the Axe Valley plotted from aerial photographs taken in the 1940s before many of the remains were ploughed flat. Many of the features are known to relate to Roman settlements in the area but there is also evidence of a subsequent medieval phase of wetland reclamation.

Nyland

1km

N

Monk Moor

Stoke Moor

Wedmore Moor

Westbury Moor

Archaeological features ——
Relict streams ····
Probably flooded areas

South-west corner of the mosaic found at Lopen in 2001. Apart from more usual geometric designs, the mosaic also features a dolphin and there is a fish elsewhere in the design. The mosaic is likely to date to the third quarter of the 4th century.

heating. These are sometimes added to quite modest buildings indicating the importance attached to each status symbol. Recent discoveries at Lopen and Dinnington have added to the picture of late-Roman wealth in this area. Both were provided with high-quality mosaics and the plan of the site at Dinnington shows that it was one of the largest in the country, comparable with well-known sites such as Bignor (Sussex) and Chedworth (Gloucestershire). In Somerset most villas form a distinct cluster within about 10km of Ilchester in the attractive hills to the north and south.

This pattern also emphasises the importance of the low-lying areas to the geography of Somerset in early periods. Although it is difficult to estimate the extent of the marshy areas it is clear that they almost cut the county in two. The importance of the position of Ilchester, where these wetlands end, is clear. Recent work has shown that land was being reclaimed in the Roman period in the areas around Brent Knoll. The presence of substantial buildings, including a villa at Lakehouse Farm, in very low-lying situations indicates that the rivers must have been embanked to prevent flooding. This reclamation is also implied by the extensive areas of Roman field system recorded in the Axe Valley, further inland.

Further to the south, in the area around Gold Corner, salt was being produced, the evidence surviving as mounds of briquetage (rough pottery containers used to evaporate brine). The presence of this industry indicates a salt marsh environment and therefore no embankments and reclamation in this area.

INDUSTRY

Pottery was being made at Shepton Mallet where kilns producing Severn Valley Ware were discovered during the building of the Anglo-Bavarian brewery in 1864. These kilns seem to have flourished around the end of the 1st century and into the 2nd and may have been serving a military market in Wales and the north.

At Charterhouse and other sites on Mendip lead was mined. Recent excavations have shown that a small fort was constructed very soon after the conquest and that abandoned mines were being filled in before the end of the 1st century. There is evidence from this site, and others, that lead was being mined in the Iron Age and that the Romans took over and expanded an existing industry. The mines appear to have been under military control at first because ingots stamped IMP VESPASIANI AUG, dating them to the reign of Vespasian (AD 69–79), have been found. After this the mines seem to have reverted to civilian working and the fort was abandoned. To the west of the mining area there appears to have been a substantial settlement. Aerial photographs show streets and compounds similar to those excavated at Shepton Mallet and an earthwork survives which may be an amphitheatre.

The extent of Roman iron working has recently been recognised in the Blackdown Hills where sites have been located and some excavated (in Devon) showing again an early start to an extensive industry. An association between iron working debris and Roman pottery has been known for many years on the Brendon Hills and Exmoor at sites such as Clatworthy and Syndercombe (where the name is indicative). Recent work in the later iron working areas around the so-called Roman Lode has shown that some of the workings there are dateable to the Roman period and suggest a sizeable industry.

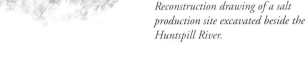

Reconstruction drawing of a salt production site excavated beside the Huntspill River.

In general, however, the majority of the population (which may have been as high as 5–10 % of modern levels in the later Roman period) would have lived by farming and Somerset would have been a predominantly agricultural area, much as it is now. The main difference in the settlement pattern would have been a lack of villages, which with a few exceptions (for example at Catsgore) seem to have developed after the Roman period.

THE LATER ROMAN PERIOD

During the 3rd century, after Britain had been part of the Roman empire for 200 years, the character of the empire changed. This was viewed at the time as a crisis but it is not clear how the archaeological evidence from Britain is related to the historical events. The underlying cause of this change appears to have been the end of expansion and the stabilisation of the empire within fixed boundaries. This changed the balance of power, both military and economic,

Lead pig found at Chewton Mendip. It bears the name of Emperor Vespasian, dating the pig to the period AD 69–79.

Bronze figurines from the temple on Lamyatt Beacon, Bruton, depicting Roman gods Hercules, Minerva, Mars and Mercury.

much of the town may have been given over to the gardens of the large houses. Conversely, at this time there was major expenditure on the building of defences at Ilchester. The villas of the elite saw continued investment and the large cemeteries suggest a continued central role for the town in the wider community.

It was not only at the palatial villas that money was being spent in the countryside. There was an increase in the construction of simple rectangular stone buildings, for example to the north of Shapwick, and of small villas, for example at Spaxton. These may have been subsidiary buildings on larger estates or they may reflect smaller landowners gaining sufficient wealth to invest in stone buildings.

Possibly for tax reasons, the focus of economic activity evidently moved from the civitas capitals to smaller towns, often on the borders of the civitates. Shepton Mallet

Bronze figurine of a Lar, or household god, found at Castle Cary.

between the core of the empire and its fringes. The army became more involved in politics and the emperor more dependent on it. Economically, the lack of wealth gained by conquest and investment in new provinces combined with the increasing cost of the army, lead to increased taxes and an inflationary spiral. This hit the ruling classes hardest, making them less keen to fulfil their traditional roles in the running of the towns. Taxes, which had been collected in the towns in coin, were increasingly collected in kind, which further reduced the economic role of the towns.

The old system of local rulers running the civitas and collecting taxes in return for local power was replaced by a state bureaucracy that used tax incentives to force the same people to run the system of requisitions and taxation in kind.

In Britain these changes seem to have resulted in a decrease in the economic vitality of the civitas capitals (which probably included Ilchester by this time) and a growth in activity in the countryside. Public buildings in towns were abandoned or used for other purposes and

was one such location where the construction of stone buildings suggests increasing wealth.

Another feature of the later Roman period is the appearance of temples on several hilltops across the county. Temples seem to have been established in towns during the early period and some rural temples are known in the east of the country. No early temples are known in Somerset and all seem to have been established in the late 3rd and 4th centuries. The construction of these temples may have been an attempt by pagans to display the importance of their beliefs in the face of the spread of a new religion: Christianity. At Brean Down, Lamyatt Beacon and Henley Wood the temples appear to have been finally destroyed and replaced by possible Christian chapels.

Part of a hoard of silver coins and pieces of hacksilver (melted down silver cut into pieces with a hammer and chisel) found at West Bagborough. It was buried in c. AD 365.

CHRISTIANITY

Much consideration has been given to the spread of Christianity in the Roman world but it is still extremely difficult to recognise because of its secretive beginnings, lack of specialised buildings and uninformative burial practices. The picture in Britain is additionally confused by the ending of imperial control, which happened at around the same time. No Roman church sites are known in Somerset (with the possible exception of the east to west aligned buildings replacing pagan temples mentioned above) but in several places, circumstantial evidence suggests the presence of Christian communities. At Ilchester the burials from a large cemetery established late in the 4th century at Northover House are believed to be Christian and may presage the later focus at St Andrew's Church, Northover, which became a Saxon minster. At Shepton Mallet separate small cemeteries of oriented and north–south aligned graves may indicate Christians and pagans living side by side.

BRITONS AND SAXONS

THE END OF IMPERIAL ADMINISTRATION

The period between the withdrawal of Roman imperial control from Britain and the establishment of the Anglo-Saxon kingdoms is one with which both archaeology and history have problems. The traditional picture, from the time of Bede (*c.* 731), has been of invasion and conquest by peoples from over the North Sea and the pushing of the British into the 'Celtic West'.

Whereas in earlier periods the lack of historical sources is obviously accepted, the presence in this period of a few has encouraged a belief that our understanding ought to be both more full and to be fitted into a historical framework. The sources that we possess are, however, both scarce and obscure and it is only by combining the information from archaeology and history, and studying the Roman origins of the landscape and its subsequent medieval development, that it is possible to say something about the period. Even the fact that the period has no accepted name is indicative of the problems and perceptions surrounding it (Dark Age, Post-Roman, Sub-Roman, Early Christian, Early Medieval, Old Welsh, Late Antique and Early, Middle and Late Saxon are all in use, and each categorises a different modern approach).

At the end of the Roman period most of Somerset would have lain in the *civitas* of the Durotriges, possibly in a subdivision of the *civitas* based on Ilchester. How long this civil administration continued is uncertain but some evidence, such as that of St Patrick who refers to his father as a town councillor, suggests a date in the middle of the 5th century for some areas. A hundred years later, when Gildas was writing, kings ruled all the areas that he mentions, although there are hints that he is merely singling out the kings for criticism and may have lived in an area of different political structures himself.

Gildas is the most useful of the early writers, particularly as it has been suggested that he was writing in the Somerset or Dorset areas in the middle of the 6th century. He has been used as a source for information on the 5th century from the time of Bede, but it is the incidental information on the 6th century that is perhaps more informative. Gildas writes in a wholly Christian context, and one that he sees as degenerating. He writes in Latin and appears to have had a civil (as opposed to an ecclesiastical) education. This all suggests continuity of Roman traditions and institutions.

Fragment of amphora made in the eastern Mediterranean and found at Cadbury Castle. Amphorae were used to import luxury commodities such as wine and olive oil in the late 5th and early 6th centuries.

There was also continuing contact with the late Roman world centred on Byzantium (modern Istanbul in Turkey). Some of the few diagnostic finds from sites of this period are imported pottery vessels from the Mediterranean. These are rare but found over much of the west of Britain, often at defended sites within reach of the coast. In Somerset, sherds have been found at Cadbury Castle, Cannington, Glastonbury and, recently, at Carhampton and Athelney. Recent work has suggested that this pottery may be a sign of diplomatic missions from Byzantium as part of a plan to re-establish the empire.

Cadbury Castle is one of the most remarkable sites of this period in Britain. The excavations in the 1960s showed that the hilltop, which had been occupied from prehistoric times, was refortified with a timber and stone wall over 1km long and with at least one elaborate gate. This work clearly required the mobilisation of a large amount of labour, and this together with the presence of imported pottery suggests a political centre. It appears to have been located to control

Reconstruction drawing of the interior of the 6th-century hall at Cadbury Castle.

the road from the east and is close to both Ilchester, which it might have replaced, and to the important early religious centre at Lanprobi (near Sherborne, Dorset). There is similar evidence of very large-scale defensive works in the north of historic Somerset where the Wansdyke appears to be marking a boundary against penetration along the Avon.

The limited nature of the evidence surviving on Glastonbury Tor makes it difficult to interpret but it may represent an aristocratic residence or more likely, in view of the later history of the site, an early monastic foundation, perhaps a hermitage associated with the site of Lantokai at Street.

The recently-discovered site at Carhampton is more enigmatic. Here, at the eastern end of the village, Mediterranean imported pottery was discovered at a low-lying site together with evidence for metalworking. To the west lay a later cemetery possibly associated with a chapel recorded in the 16th century as dedicated to St Carantoc. The situation of the site, the two churches, the links to an early saint and the later royal ownership of Carhampton may suggest a monastic site, under royal patronage. The location of the royal centre is unknown but Dunster Tor is an obvious candidate as may be Bats Castle or Cannington hillfort.

Cemeteries are known at Brean Down and Cannington

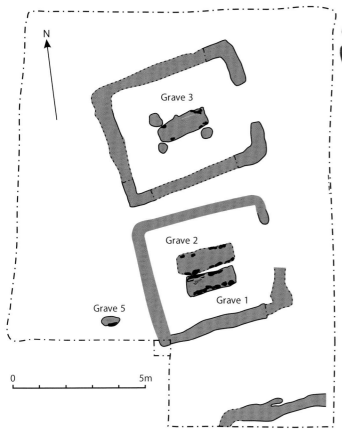

The distinctive burials from Stoneage Barton. It seems likely that the enclosure ditches held the foundations for small buildings – each with an entrance on the east.

where a large cemetery was excavated in 1962–3. This originated in the 4th century and appeared to have developed from the focus of a late Roman shrine and to have continued into the 8th century. The cemetery lay close to Cannington hillfort, which may have continued in use at this time. A similar cemetery is known from Henley Wood (North Somerset) adjacent to a late Roman temple and close to Cadbury Congresbury, another hillfort that was certainly occupied in the 5th to 6th centuries.

A different form of cemetery has recently been found at Stoneage Barton, near Cothelstone. Here, as well as simple burials, several graves were discovered surrounded by a shallow square ditch with an entrance gap on the east.

These distinctive graves are known from only a handful of other sites in England and Wales and seem to be continuing a Roman funerary practice seen, for example, at Poundbury, Dorchester. Very little bone survived but a radiocarbon date indicated burial in the mid-7th century.

The later history of some other sites suggests that they can be identified as important places in this period. Among these is Cheddar where the parish church lies on top of an extensive Roman site. A recent radiocarbon date from the mid-6th century indicates continuing activity and the site later became a Saxon and Norman royal centre.

THE ANGLO-SAXONS

The mechanism by which British kingdoms became incorporated into the Anglo-Saxon kingdom of Wessex is still unclear. Gildas tells us that the first Saxon settlers were invited to Britain as mercenaries, a common late Roman practice. Saxons appear in the archaeological record in the upper Thames valley in the early fifth century and historical information suggests that these people, the Gewisse, formed the core from which Wessex grew. Interestingly, their legendary early rulers had anglicised British names, which may suggest a complex origin for the kingdom. Much of the early historical material, principally the Anglo-Saxon Chronicle, is extremely suspect for the 5th and 6th centuries, but the picture that is painted is one of expansion by the Gewisse, through conquest of both Saxon and British groups, to form Wessex, and rivalry with the emerging kingdom of Mercia to the north. This is likely to be concealing a more complex picture, perhaps including marriage alliances, which might not appear in the 'heroic' story presented by the Chronicle.

Somerset, to the west of the great forest of

Silver hand-pin dating to the 5th-6th century. It was found at Long Sutton.

Reconstruction of the royal halls and ancillary buildings at Cheddar in the 10th century.

Selwood, appears to have fallen under West Saxon control in the later 7th century when charter evidence from Glastonbury and Sherborne indicates Saxon royal patronage. The *Life of St Boniface*, additionally, indicates an English abbot at Exeter by 680. The laws of Ine (688–726) acknowledge both British and English subjects, with similar social orders but with the British having half the wergild (compensation) value of the English. The fact that they had a wergild at all shows that they were normal (not slave) subjects of the king and by the time of Alfred's laws the discrimination had vanished.

The archaeological evidence for the period before the 10th century is extremely limited as a lack of diagnostic artefacts makes sites hard to recognise. Work by Michael

Costen has suggested a landscape of large estates in the hands of the king and nobles with on-going donations to the church. Internally the estates appear to have comprised smaller units, some with specialised functions. Royal control was exercised from the estate centres, which were visited

Part of an early 9th-century cross-shaft found in 1866 below the floor between the nave and chancel of All Saints' church, West Camel.

Mid to late 11th-century panel bearing a carving of St Peter found in a garden at Dowlish Wake. Its place of origin is unknown but it is likely to have been a religious house in Somerset.

DEFENCE AGAINST THE VIKINGS

The historical record for the 9th century is dominated by the attacks of Viking bands and armies. Somerset was open to raids from Vikings based in Ireland, and the Anglo-Saxon Chronicle records attacks on Carhampton in the 830s. In 845 a great victory over the Vikings is recorded at the mouth of the River Parrett and this seems to have discouraged further large-scale raids. The eastern part of Wessex continued to be attacked by large forces principally from Denmark. In 870 a far greater threat emerged, when the 'great heathen army' that had defeated the Northumbrians and East Angles turned its attention to Wessex. After at least nine major battles the Vikings were bought off by King Alfred and withdrew northwards. They returned in 878, surprising Alfred at Chippenham shortly after Christmas. The eastern part of Wessex appears to have submitted to Guthrum, the Viking king, and Alfred fled towards his estates in Somerset. From here he rallied sufficient forces to defeat Guthrum who agreed to convert to Christianity and was baptised at Aller.

The Saxon response to these Viking attacks can be seen in the establishment of fortifications, possibly starting in the reign of Alfred's predecessor Æthelbald.

periodically by the court as it moved around the kingdom, but otherwise run by officials. This system removed the difficulty of sending taxes, and the produce of the estate, to the king. One of the most important of these royal centres is likely to have been Somerton, after which the county is evidently named, but no archaeological evidence for this has been found. Excavations at the site of Cheddar, however, showed a sequence of halls, chapels and ancillary buildings dating from at least the 9th century and which was a royal possession until 1230 when acquired by the Bishop of Bath and Wells.

Three early monastic sites are known, namely Glastonbury, Muchelney and Frome, which were in existence by the end of the 7th century. Only Glastonbury, however, was successful in gaining large estates. The arrangement of minster churches and dependent chapels serving the population, seen in the later Saxon period, is likely to have grown from an original pattern of estate churches.

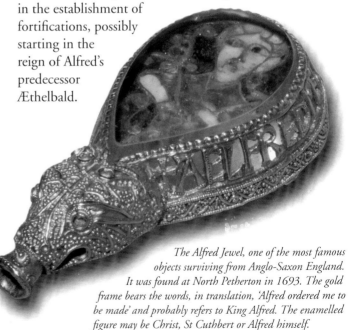

The Alfred Jewel, one of the most famous objects surviving from Anglo-Saxon England. It was found at North Petherton in 1693. The gold frame bears the words, in translation, 'Alfred ordered me to be made' and probably refers to King Alfred. The enamelled figure may be Christ, St Cuthbert or Alfred himself.

Alfred the Great, by George Vertue, 1732. The engraving depicts King Alfred and events surrounding his defeat of the Danes in AD 878.

Bone plaque with incised interlaced decoration found during excavations at Cadbury Castle. The plaque, which dates to the 11th century, was probably attached to a wooden box or casket.

In the Late Saxon and Norman periods there was a series of mints across Somerset where silver pennies were struck. The coins in this group derive from the Taunton mint and were issued in the names of Cnut, Edward the Confessor, Harold II, William I and Henry I.

In Somerset 'burhs' were established at Axbridge, Langport, Lyng and Watchet where they appear to be based on royal estates at Cheddar, Somerton, Athelney and Carhampton (or Cannington) and to be guarding against attacks from the sea. Unlike some other burhs of this period the Somerset ones have produced little archaeological evidence. There is argument over the exact site of Axbridge, and excavations in Langport and Lyng (where the sites of defensive banks are known) have produced almost no evidence of internal settlement. Only at Watchet have excavations shown the sequence of the defences, which incorporated a stone wall. Even here, however, the only features discovered in the interior were of Post-Medieval date.

Other towns appeared at around this time and some, because of more suitable locations, superseded the burhs. By the time of Domesday Book (1086), Taunton, Bruton, Ilchester, Langport, Milborne Port, Milverton, Axbridge, Crewkerne, South Petherton, Watchet, Frome and

Ilminster appear to have had urban characteristics. Very little archaeological evidence for most of these sites has, however, been recovered, so it is difficult to characterise their nature. The Viking attacks resumed in the reign of Æthelred II who adopted similar policies to those of Alfred and constructed a new burh on the earlier site at Cadbury Castle. The excavations showed that a rampart faced with mortared stone was constructed around the top of hill together with at least one monumental gate. In 1009–10, when there are indications that the project had not yet been completed, coin evidence shows that the Ilchester mint was moved to Cadbury Castle. The ultimately successful Danish king, Cnut, closed the mint and the moneyers moved to the towns of Bruton, Crewkerne and Ilchester in 1019.

Ninth-century gold finger ring found at Maperton.

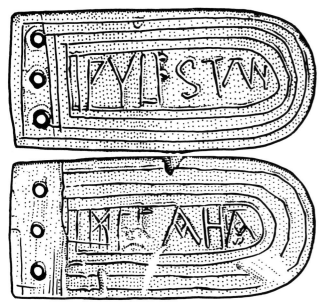

Lead strap-end found near Crewkerne. It is insribed with the words which read, in translation, "Wulfstan owns me", 10th-11th century.

THE MIDDLE AGES

INTRODUCTION

In 1086, twenty years after they first arrived in Somerset, the Normans produced their remarkable tax inventory known as Domesday Book. This document records the names and details of hundreds of Somerset manors and estates. Although the location of many Domesday sites can be difficult to correlate with modern places, it is clear that by the late 11th century the basic settlement pattern of the county was already in existence, a pattern which still influences where people live and work today. Several towns and many villages were already established and operating as market centres, as well as places for religious worship and specialist services. During the 12th and early 13th centuries written evidence increases our knowledge of the county and helps to establish some key dates in the development of medieval Somerset but it rarely provides evidence of everyday activities. Only through archaeological research can we create a more detailed picture of where people lived and worked and what they made and discarded.

CASTLES

The arrival of the Normans in Somerset was marked not least by the establishment of castles. One of the most dramatic sites they chose was at Dunster, where William de Mohun, a powerful Norman baron who reputedly fought at the Battle of Hastings, created his castle on a commanding spur of land. By the early years of the 12th century many castles had been constructed, such as those at Nether Stowey, Over Stowey, Castle Cary, Fenny Castle, Stoke sub Hamdon and Farleigh Hungerford. Others were evidently built during the Anarchy of King Stephen's reign (1135–54), while Bridgwater castle was created under a licence of 1200 and Nunney was built as late as the 1370s. The earliest Norman castles were of 'motte and bailey' design, and consisted of a large earth mound (the motte, originally with a timber tower on top) and an area defended by banks and ditches (the bailey, originally filled with buildings). One of the best-preserved castles of this type is Castle Neroche to the south of Taunton where a prehistoric fort was adapted to form the bailey. Castle Cary's motte and bailey castle was probably built in the early 12th century on the site of an 11th-century ringwork.

Reconstruction drawing of the castle at Bridgwater with the medieval bridge that gave the town its name in the foreground. Apart from part of the water gate and a length of wall, nothing survives of the castle above ground.

Mid-12th century silver spoon found in the keep area of Taunton Castle.

The ruins of Farleigh Hungerford Castle by W W Wheatley, 1842.

Excavations in 1890 revealed the foundations of a large keep 24m square. It was probably destroyed after the Anarchy, during which it was besieged twice. By contrast Stogursey Castle had towers added to its curtain wall in the 13th century and Taunton Castle was substantially enlarged and altered over a period of several centuries. Smaller castles, such as Nether Stowey, had keeps suitable only as guard posts and were abandoned well before the end of the Middle Ages.

Towns

Domesday Book records only twelve towns in Somerset. By the end of the 13th century, however, over 40 places in the county contained burgage plots – the regular parcels of land typically laid out in a town – together with other indications of urban status. Archaeological work, such as that recently undertaken at the centre of Taunton, has shown that this was a period of expansion. One of the earliest examples of urban growth in Somerset is at Ilchester where excavations have revealed that extensive quarrying of the Roman remains took place from the 10th century onwards and new town walls, with four entrance gates,

The Market Place, Wells, by Edward Dayes, c. 1790. The buildings on the left are the 'New Works' built by Bishop Bekynton in 1451. In the foreground is Bekynton's Conduit which supplied the Market Place with water brought from the bishop's wells. The conduit was replaced in 1793.

were built in the early 13th century. There is evidence of a flourishing medieval community with numerous craftsmen, including goldsmiths. The town also had several churches and religious houses, including a Dominican friary. By the 14th century, however, Ilchester was in serious decline, possibly because it had temporarily lost the county courts and gaol to Somerton. The population dwindled, the churches were gradually abandoned, and parishes were united.

Other towns not only expanded but also successfully maintained their prosperity, and there is evidence of much building activity in the later Middle Ages. Though Taunton has lost most of its early domestic buildings, excavations in the late 20th century revealed evidence of its medieval fabric, including foundations of the 15th-century Guildhall and of the alehouses and shops that increasingly encroached on the market place. In a town such as Bruton, where many older buildings survive, archaeological recording and dendrochronology are helping to shape our knowledge of the development of timber-framed structures. Although it is impossible to be certain of the ranking of towns in the Middle Ages, by the 14th century Wells was probably the largest in Somerset. It still has many medieval domestic buildings, and is one of the best places in Somerset to see standing evidence of medieval planning, notably in the 15th-century Vicars' Close and in the less well known New Works of 1451 beside the market place.

RURAL SETTLEMENTS

The origins of many smaller settlements are gradually being revealed by archaeological excavation. At Milborne Port excavations next to the parish church in advance of redevelopment revealed extensive and well-preserved remains of ditches, pits and buildings ranging in date from the 11th to the 14th centuries. The challenge of understanding the change from a dispersed settlement pattern in the Roman period to the villages we see in medieval Somerset still remains, but the process is becoming clearer as more archaeological work is undertaken.

One of the key sites for Somerset is the parish of Shapwick. Ten years of archaeological work in the parish,

A late 18th-century view by T Bonner of Glastonbury Abbey's manor house at Shapwick with the abbey's barn to the left. In the medieval period one of the main streets of the village led up to the, then moated, house and was lined with houses – all these were removed to create an open parkland after the dissolution. The barn was also later demolished.

undertaken as part of the Shapwick Project, has located a series of discrete Roman settlements, one of which became the first site of the church. The present village appears to have been a deliberate foundation by Glastonbury Abbey, and is based on a ladder-like grid of roads to the west of the church. Presumably the tenants of outlying settlements were moved into the village as part of the abbey's agricultural and tenurial improvements. Historical sources indicate that the present church (built 1331–2) is a later addition to the village, although a space may have been left in the plan for it from the outset. The manor complex may have been moved into the 'new' village in the later 13th century. The vernacular buildings of Shapwick have been studied in detail, and the work of the Somerset Vernacular Buildings Research Group and other partners has in general added enormously to our understanding of the county's building stock, in both rural and urban contexts. The earliest known vernacular building, dated by dendrochronology, is at Garnivals Week in Milverton parish, where the hall roof includes timbers felled in 1287.

Though Shapwick has been intensively studied both by historians and archaeologists, our knowledge of the development of other villages, particularly ones that were not controlled by monastic landlords, is generally poor. Even less well understood are the isolated farms and small hamlets of west Somerset. Tax documents such as the Lay Subsidy of 1344 can be used to confirm the existence of some of these settlements, and their locations can often be identified. Despite Mick Aston's pioneering work in west Somerset, little further work has been carried out to study their transition into single farms, often now deserted, and little work has been carried out in the rest of the county. Somerset is an important place for these types of study because it falls across the transition zone between the dispersed settlement pattern, evident in the west of the county, to the more Midland pattern of villages and open fields which can be seen in south and east Somerset. Archaeological research on medieval field systems is very fragmentary but recent mapping of aerial photographs is starting to plot the distribution of ridge and furrow

Earthwork remains of one of the later buildings at Nether Adber deserted village. The positions of two doorways can be seen in the long walls.

earthworks. Excavation and analysis is awaited.

The south-east of the county contains many deserted medieval villages, such as Nether Adber near Marston Magna. The reasons for the desertion of these sites have been much debated, and although the Black Death may sometimes have had a role to play, so too did longer-term economic changes. At Nether Adber, a study of the earthworks shows that houses stood in plots around a triangular village green as well as along side roads. A manorial site lay to the north but has been flattened. Later, some of the plots seem to have been amalgamated, suggesting a reduced (but perhaps wealthier) population. There is now only one house.

Other structures also left a significant mark on the rural landscape. Watermills existed throughout the county during the Middle Ages and pre-dated the arrival of windmills, which are first recorded in the 12th century. In addition, extensive remains of sluices, clyces, weirs, floodbanks, millraces, and drainage systems are known, but accurate dating evidence for many of these features is lacking. The existence of timber stakes, associated with inter-tidal fishing, can be seen all along the Somerset coast from Porlock towards Brean Down. Detailed examination of timber posts in Bridgwater Bay has now confirmed that some of these fishing features date back to the 10th century.

Minehead Bay in the early 19th century. The view would have been similar in the medieval period with numerous fish traps and weirs together with small vessels trading and fishing in the Bristol Channel.

PARISH CHURCHES

One of the most important institutions in medieval society was the church. There are over 350 medieval parish churches in Somerset, which together form an extraordinary repository of historic and archaeological evidence. Most parish churches have occupied the same site for over a thousand years, but their origins are in general obscure. Some appear to have been built on or near Roman sites, as at Shapwick (old church) or Ilchester Northover, though whether this shows continuity of settlement, or just that a Roman ruin was thought appropriate for the site of a church, is not clear. Street church, like many others, appears to have been built on an early site and may, like the church

at Milborne Port, have been in existence before the Norman Conquest. The origins of some churches are known in greater detail. The church at North Cadbury, for example, was completely rebuilt during the late 14th or early 15th century, the tower by the rector John Ferour (d. 1408) and the rest before 1417 by Elizabeth, Lady Botreaux, to house a college of priests. At Stogursey the church was in origin part of a priory founded in the early 12th century by Lonlay Abbey in Normandy, becoming the parish church when the priory was suppressed in about 1440. A similar situation occurred at Dunster where the former priory became the parish church following the dissolution in 1539.

Archaeological investigation in and around churches

Northover Church by W W Wheatley in 1847. Although no early fabric can be seen in the present building it lies at the edge of the Roman cemetery to the north of Ilchester and is a good candidate for continuity from a chapel over an important Christian burial.

during building work continues to reveal evidence of earlier features such as the two large boundary ditches at St John's, Wellington, that appear to pre-date the nave. Excavations at Curry Rivel revealed a very fine 14th-century grave slab depicting a tonsured priest complete with robes and chalice. Investigation and recording at several parish churches, such as All Saints, Holy Trinity, or St James's, Taunton, have revealed archaeological evidence of how these medieval churches expanded to become the aisled buildings that survive today. Medieval Somerset also contained many free-standing chapels and chantries. Some, such as the chapel

Students from the University of Bristol excavating to the north of St John's church, Wellington. In the foreground is a late Saxon boundary ditch, which can be seen running below the later medieval churchyard wall and then under the church itself.

of St Thomas between the villages of North and South Cadbury, survived by being converted to domestic use but most have left little trace. The 13th-century chapel of Our Lady at Adscombe, Over Stowey, for example, has now largely been reduced to wall footings.

Somerset's largest surviving medieval church is, of course, the cathedral of St Andrew at Wells. Begun in the period 1175–85, and consecrated in 1239, the cathedral was the first building in the world to display the new Gothic style in all its fullness. It remains an outstanding masterpiece of European medieval art. Excavations in 1978–80, directed by Warwick Rodwell, revealed the apsed east end of the earlier Saxon cathedral. The foundations of that building, which was evidently some 300 feet long, run diagonally under the present cloister range.

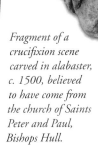

Gravestone from St Andrew's Church, Curry Rivel, showing a late 13th-century priest in full mass vestments and holding a chalice. The stone was reused as a doorslab and recovered during repairs in 2004.

Fragment of a crucifixion scene carved in alabaster, c. 1500, believed to have come from the church of Saints Peter and Paul, Bishops Hull.

MONASTERIES

The development of monasticism is well represented in Somerset, and numerous religious houses were established in the county. Dominant both locally and regionally, Glastonbury Abbey was one of the richest monasteries in the country by the end of the 12th century. Like other large houses, it had a major influence on the landscape of the county, controlling settlement development and agricultural improvements across considerable areas. Together with the abbeys of Muchelney and Athelney, and the cathedral at Wells, Glastonbury Abbey was particularly influential in the Somerset levels and moors, an area containing some of the best examples of medieval drainage and land reclamation anywhere in England. Notable surviving features include the Abbot of Glastonbury's 14th-century fish house at Meare, which stands by the site of the former Meare Pool, once part of a complex system of watercourses and fish weirs.

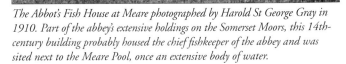

The Abbot's Fish House at Meare photographed by Harold St George Gray in 1910. Part of the abbey's extensive holdings on the Somerset Moors, this 14th-century building probably housed the chief fishkeeper of the abbey and was sited next to the Meare Pool, once an extensive body of water.

The ruins of Glastonbury Abbey after a drawing by Coplestone Warr Bampfylde, 1746. Once the wealthiest monastic house in England, the abbey had a profound effect on the development of the landscape of Somerset.

Glastonbury also had a leading role in draining the moors east of the Parrett. A series of walls was constructed, several of which, such as Burrow Wall and Baltmoor Wall, survive impressively today. On the outskirts of Glastonbury itself are the traces of one of the earliest examples of a 'canal' yet found in the country. This canal linked Glastonbury Abbey directly to the River Brue and was no doubt an important supply route for construction materials and goods into the town. Radiocarbon dating of timber posts associated with this canal suggest that it may have been cut during the 10th century, perhaps when St Dunstan was abbot.

Smaller monastic houses, such as Burtle Priory, on the Levels between Wedmore and the Polden Hills, also affected the character and management of the immediately surrounding countryside. In a few cases monastic buildings belonging to these smaller houses have survived. At Witham Friary the 12th-century church for the lay brothers remains. A number of important monastic barns have survived, including Glastonbury Abbey's barns at Doulting, Pilton and Glastonbury itself, and the recently-identified barn at West Lyng belonging to Atheleney Abbey.

Aerial view of Athelney Hill with the geophysical survey results superimposed, showing the buried remains of the Benedictine abbey. Further archaeological remains are known in the field to the left. Before extensive drainage, both fields would have formed an island connected by a causeway to nearby Lyng.

Medieval burials at Taunton Priory uncovered in 2005. The Priory, like its predecessor which stood in the area of Castle Green, had a monopoly on burials from a wide area in, and around, the town. Large numbers of skeletons have been found at both sites.

Medieval monasteries also affected the development of towns, for example at Ilchester where much of the south-west of the town was the precinct of a Dominican Friary. There was also an Augustinian nunnery within the town as well as seven churches and chapels. Excavations in Bridgwater in 2003 on the site of St John's Friary revealed the robbed-out remains of numerous medieval walls giving a clear indication of the scale and size of some of the medieval buildings associated with the priory. In 2004 an even more spectacular discovery was made in the area of Taunton's Augustinian Priory. Redevelopment near St James's Church revealed the edge of the medieval cloister and the robbed-out nave and aisles of the Priory Church. In addition to the wall foundations, numerous fragments of worked stone, medieval window glass and tile fragments were recovered, together with more than 200 burials. Analysis of the skeletal remains from the priory should provide an important insight into the life and death of the medieval population of Taunton and the surrounding estates.

SECULAR LORDS

Secular lords, as well as monastic ones, were a dominant factor in controlling the development of the landscape, the layout of fields, the extent of woodlands and the creation of deer parks, gardens, fish ponds, moats and manor houses. Many aspects of the medieval rural landscape created by such landowners survive as field monuments in the county. Somerset has over 80 identified medieval deer parks. Other archaeological features such as rabbit warrens, with their characteristic 'pillow mounds', survive at Bruton and other sites but few of these features have been excavated. Many of the smaller landowners surrounded their houses with moats (a fashion perhaps inspired by the use of water defences around castles) and several survive in the east of the county. At Marston Magna a substantial moated site and fishpond survive as earthworks, but no trace of buildings has been

The moated manor house site at Marston Magna with the church in the background. The earthworks were later used to form a formal garden for the house on the far left.

confirmed despite recent geophysical surveys. Excavations at Spargrove Manor revealed the waterlogged timber remains of the medieval bridge that linked the manor house with the courtyard. These timbers were dated by dendrochronology to 1289–90 and are linked with the Sansares family. Recent work at Kilve by English Heritage has shown that the so-called Chantry Chapel was in fact part of the extensive manor house complex that occupied the site to the north of the parish church.

COMMUNICATIONS

Communications and trade made use of a network of roads and tracks, many of which are apparent today as substantial sunken ways. These hollow ways are an important characteristic of our historic landscape and survive in particular abundance in the soft sandstones of south-east Somerset and in west Somerset. There has been limited archaeological investigation of early roads of this kind and further analysis might provide evidence of their origins. River crossings were also of key importance. The earliest crossings were fords such as that at Allerford on Exmoor, but in the medieval period many bridges were built. Excavations at Cotford Bridge, near Cotford St Luke, revealed a fording point below a late medieval bridge. Archaeological investigations at Dowlish Wake packhorse bridge showed the existence of early paving below the later medieval structure. Rivers were not always obstacles and many were also used for communication. The River Parrett formed an important artery, allowing the transport of goods from the sea to Bridgwater and then inland to Langport. Goods were also transported in the other direction, for example building stone from Ham Hill.

The base of a wooden bridge crossing the moat at Spargrove Manor, Batcombe. Dendrochronology has shown that one of the timbers was felled in 1289 and the bridge survived until the late 14th century when it was replaced by a stone causeway.

In addition to the ports at Bridgwater and Minehead, small harbours were established at such places as Watchet, Porlock and Highbridge. The smaller ships of the Middle Ages also made good use of tiny creeks such as Kilve Pill, and in the 14th century corn was shipped to Ireland from Combwich. Several of these now abandoned ports have considerable archaeological potential.

MINES AND MINERALS

There are extensive mineral resources in Somerset and stone quarrying has a long history. Extensive quarrying was undertaken at Doulting for the construction of Glastonbury Abbey and Wells Cathedral, and many other quarries operated during the Middle Ages. Ham Hill was extensively quarried and the use of Ham stone is evident throughout the county and beyond. Tilestones were also quarried in Somerset and lias paving was dug at Ivythorn Hill near Street during the 14th century. Recent archaeological research on Exmoor and the Blackdown Hills has shown that mining for iron ore and the smelting of iron was much more common in these areas than previously thought. Other minerals were also exploited, one of the most important being lead from Mendip, particularly from the Priddy Mineries around Charterhouse on Mendip. Extensive mining remains survive at Charterhouse, but they have not yet been subject to detailed archaeological survey, making it difficult to decide which areas relate to medieval working. A new survey of the Mendip AONB is now underway and this, carried out by English Heritage, will provide new evidence on the extent and character of this historic mining landscape.

Bridgwater's medieval bridge. Ports such as Bridgwater played a vital part in medieval trade as goods were much more easily transported by water than on the poor roads of the time.

MANUFACTURING INDUSTRIES

Archaeological evidence for medieval manufacturing industries in Somerset, such as leather working, tanning (Taunton), charcoal production (Exmoor), iron working (Blackdowns, Exmoor), and brewing (Bineham), is gradually appearing. Other industries such as glass manufacture, stone quarrying (Ham Hill, Doulting), lead working (Mendip), and coal mining (Coleford) have yet to be methodically examined or documented. Pottery production in Somerset is known from several sites, but few medieval pottery kilns have been excavated and reported on to modern standards. The exception to this is at Donyatt in south Somerset, where excavations have shown that pottery production continued for over 500 years. Pottery is one of the most common artefacts found on medieval sites and recent scientific examination of pottery fabrics is starting to piece together the story of clay sources and production sites.

Post-Medieval Somerset

Introduction

Relatively little attention has been paid to Post-Medieval archaeology in Somerset, and there are few extensive examples of fieldwork that can be used as keys to our interpretation of the period. Our knowledge and understanding of the artefacts produced at this time is highly dependent on archaeological sequences excavated in Bristol and Exeter during the 1970s and early 1980s, and on evidence from further afield. It is fortunate that for much of the Medieval and Post-Medieval periods large areas of modern Somerset were, in archaeological terms, parts of the hinterland of both these major cities. There have as yet been no major excavations of any of the principal urban settlements in Somerset, although the destruction of such relatively modern sites continues apace with the redevelopment of so many town and village centres. Many people have been content to interpret field monuments by relying on documentary evidence as a primary source, and by making comparisons with other field monuments, treating the collection and analysis of archaeological data as a secondary but not necessarily confirmatory source of evidence. The potential for using archaeological evidence as a primary source has been demonstrated by excavations carried out in Taunton in the 1970s. Few structures were recorded but analysis of the contents of cess and rubbish pits has given us rare insights into life in this period. The study of human intestinal parasites in a pit dated to the 16th century is a good example.

Hammet Street, Taunton, begun in 1788. Part of the new approach to designed townscapes in the 18th century, Hammet Street cuts through the medieval plan of Taunton to provide a view of the church of St Mary Magdalene and is lined with classically inspired buildings.

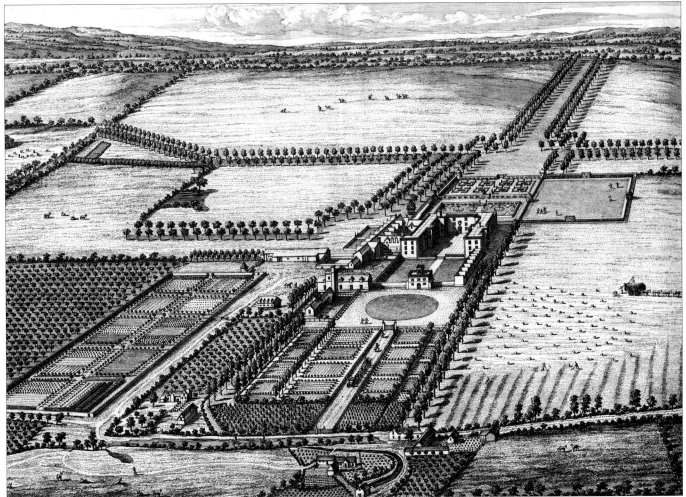

Orchard House, seat of the Portman family at Orchard Portman, by Johannes Kip, after a drawing by Leonard Knyff, 1707. The medieval manor house had been replaced by a large complex of builings, surrouned by formal gardens and parkland. The house was finally demolished in about 1843.

THE LANDSCAPE

The archaeological evidence demonstrates that the period was one of radical material cultural change, particularly influenced in the 16th and 17th centuries from the Low Countries, and towards the end of the period open to direct influence from the wider world. The landscape itself is the most comprehensive indicator of the scale of this change. By the end of the period, the rural landscape appears to have been one of enclosure except for the limestone plateaux where open fields seem still to have prevailed and for the high moorland of Exmoor and the Brendon Hills and the low moorland of the wetlands. The task of enclosing the wetlands continued with limited schemes of canalisation of the Parrett and Tone and drainage schemes such as those near the mouth of the Axe (1597–1640) and south of Langport. The construction of King's Sedgemoor Drain in 1791–95 to divert the course of the river Cary was the beginning of the final phase of extensive drainage and enclosure. So far, none of the distinctive artefacts mentioned by historical sources, such as Marshall in his *Rural Economy of the West of England* (1796), and associated with this phase of agricultural improvement in the county – pointed shovels, ploughs, wagons, etc – have survived from this period to be recorded. Big country houses also had their impact on the landscape, particularly through emparkment and the planning of gardens.

The urban landscape changed too. Many medieval towns were extended, most using traditional medieval suburban forms: narrow burgage plots lining linear ribbon development (East Reach in Taunton, Lyewater in Crewkerne, Garston Street in Shepton Mallet and possibly Bow Street in Langport) or more ambitiously planned grids of streets as exemplified by the Trinity development at Frome. The new late 17th-century concepts of the regular terrace ranged along broad streets or in squares came later in Bridgwater (Castle Street and King Square) and Taunton (The Crescent), decidedly influenced in their design and materials (bricks and rooftiles) by developments in Bristol. The introduction of brick (Gray's Almshouses, Taunton, 1635), plain tiles and pantiles seems to have been made in the early 17th century and these became widely used as building materials in those areas of the county where no good building stone was available nearby. Whilst bricks

Gray's Almshouses, Taunton. The earliest dated example of brick building in Somerset (1635) reflecting an increasing concern for social provision in the Post-Medieval period.

were most likely made in clamps or simple Scotch kilns such as the (probably later) example surviving at Blue Anchor, none of the distinctive tile kilns have ever been identified, let alone excavated.

Housing

The period has been characterised as the age of the Great Rebuilding and much excellent work has been carried out to record the vernacular buildings of the county, both rural and urban. Conversions of medieval houses and new buildings reflect new ideas of privacy (separate parlours and increasing numbers of bedchambers, planned, secluded gardens), comfort (glazing, hearths and chimneys) and well-being (built-in kitchens, ovens, decorative painting and plasterwork, furniture and furnishings). The period was also characterised by a proliferation of new specialist building types, especially in towns – schools, almshouses, workhouses and many other types of public building. The recording and analysis of these has been more as architectural rather than as archaeological surveys.

Churches and chapels

This period of great religious turmoil created a rich legacy. Whilst most monastic churches became redundant, most medieval parish churches were extensively and lavishly replanned and refitted to serve as Protestant places of worship. Croscombe (1616) is the most complete surviving example. A few new churches, notably the 17th-century ones at Low Ham and Wyke Champflower, were erected using medieval plan forms. But, as several surveys have shown, it was in the new building forms of

Mary Steet Meeting, Taunton.

the Great and many lesser Meeting Houses that the landscape was most radically changed. The Unitarian Meeting in Mary Street, Taunton is one of the precious few Great Meetings in Britain that has survived with its interior reasonably intact. The profusion of buildings (often rebuilt) in Bridgwater, Frome and Taunton are spectacular reminders of the wealth, diversity and strength of the Good Old Cause.

In and around these structures is the evidence of a change in burial rite. Wealthy patrons increasingly insisted on commemorating their lives with lavish monuments. With their burial vaults, they colonised the chancels of older churches or erected dedicated family aisles – pews for their exclusive use set amidst a pantheon of monuments above and spacious neatly organised vaults beneath. Good examples survive at Rodney

Affluence in the later 16th and 17th centuries resulted in an increase in the number of goldsmiths at work. This communion cup and cover were made by Henry Arnold of Taunton for St George's church, Ruishton, in c. 1574.

Stoke and Hinton St George. The less well-off colonised every other conceivable space beneath the floor for their more modest vaults and many who had to make do with the church- or chapel-yard had their plot marked with a stone or wooden marker. There is also evidence of the increasing and changing use of coffins. Good anthropomorphic lead examples can be seen at Farleigh Hungerford. Few post-medieval assemblages of burials have been archaeologically or pathologically studied in a systematic way – certainly nothing on the scale of Spitalfields in London.

Mark of South Petherton founder William Sturton II on a cauldron and a fragment of clay mould scratched with the same mark found in an excavation on the South Petherton foundry site. Bronze foundries at South Petherton and Montacute supplied a considerable proportion of the demand for cauldrons and skillets in southern England in the 17th century.

MANUFACTURING AND INDUSTRY

Archaeological evidence of industrial activity is sketchy. The important textile manufactory is attested by a scatter of sherds of the distinctive jars in which Spanish olive oil was imported to soap and cleanse the finished woollen cloth and the widespread occurrence of the tiny brass pins used for arming carding combs. More substantial evidence of extensive iron-working and smelting is currently emerging from systematic surveys of the Blackdown Hills and within Exmoor National Park. Similar survey work has recorded duck decoys in central Somerset and the fish weirs of Minehead Bay. Although nothing has survived from this period, there are later extant examples of the distinctive inshore and inland boat-building tradition in the collection of the County Museums Service and Watchet Boat Museum. Recent research on the Butler collection of bronze skillets and cauldrons and its acquisition by the County Museum revealed the unsuspected significance of Somerset founders in the 17th century. Our new knowledge of the collection illuminates earlier finds of mould material and other manufacturing debris excavated at Whirligig Lane, Taunton, and prompted the successful search for similar

material in South Petherton.

Evidence for improvements in communications is also thin. New Bridge over Horner Water at Allerford (17th century) has been cited as an example of the relatively piecemeal development of the road system. The needs of trade resulted in the appearance of local 'coinage' – the prolific production of copper tokens by local traders, especially in the periods 1649–72 and 1787–97 to satisfy the demand for low value small change.

POTTERY

It is the pottery-making industry that is perhaps best, if still very imperfectly, understood simply because pottery happens to be the most durable and prolific type of artefact surviving in archaeological contexts and tends therefore to be used as a chronological indicator, as well as evidence for trade and social life. Somerset wares reflect the dramatic change in the repertoire of the potter that marks the Post-Medieval period. Many of the new forms may be copies in a cheaper mass-produced medium of more expensive metal vessels (chafing-dishes, skillets, posset cups, plates), others

Earthenware pottery made at Donyatt - a urinal dated 1794 and a sgraffito-decorated dish commemorating the birth of conjoined twins at Isle Brewers in 1680.

of expensive exotic imports (teabowls), but many have far more utilitarian functions as containers or utensils. The pancheon – a large heavy-rimmed bowl with a pouring lip – is a classic West Country form, specifically designed for scalding cream to produce clotted cream.

With the exception of the works at Wincanton which made tin-glazed earthenwares (the well-known blue-and-white delftware) between *c.* 1735 and *c.* 1750, all the potteries known made ordinary red earthenwares using simple lead glazes. It is the particular way in which white slip is used – as sgraffito (scratched) decoration or perhaps even more distinctively (and sometimes with brown slips) as wet-slip decoration – that makes the wares of Somerset so distinctive. It should be noted that sgraffito-decorated ware used many motifs derived from tin-glazed earthenwares and ultimately European earthenwares and Chinese export porcelain. Unlike their counterparts from north Devon, however, they were always raw-glazed (not biscuit-fired before a separate gloss-firing). There is evidence that there

were broadly four sub-regions of makers, all using the extensive deposits of Mercia mudstones that occur over large areas of the county, and waste material from the making process has been identified at a number of sites:

- ❍ South Somerset/east Devon: Donyatt
- ❍ West Somerset: Dunster, Nether Stowey, Bridgwater, (?)Taunton, Wrangway, Langford Budville
- ❍ East Somerset/west Wiltshire: Wanstrow, Nunney Catch
- ❍ A more elusive type found in north Somerset and related to Bristol redwares

The production centre at Donyatt has been intensively studied and a series of kilns spanning the entire period excavated. Most of these were simple up-draught kilns

south Wales, and Verwood (Dorset), and even Border Wares from Hampshire/Surrey, have been identified. Fine wares and stonewares came from Bristol and further afield including Spain. German stonewares are common from the 17th century onwards, particularly tankards and bottles, and were even copied in earthenware at Donyatt. Good examples of groups have been published from Taunton, North Petherton, Glastonbury Abbey and Cleeve Abbey. By far the most exotic, because of the large proportion of Chinese export porcelain (and wine bottles), is a late 18th-century group excavated behind the museum in the Close at Wells.

THE CIVIL WAR AND MONMOUTH REBELLION

Somerset did not normally figure centre-stage in the defence of the realm. Most of its castles were dilapidated or used for non-military purposes when the Civil War

The kiln behind the Luttrell Arms at Dunster.

probably with a temporary capping of potsherds removed after every firing. The remarkable structure in the backyard of the Luttrell Arms in Dunster is a rare example of a more sophisticated design with closed top and conical chimney (a type later commonly known in Bridgwater as a 'pinny' or pinnacle kiln). It was built in 1759 and is probably the earliest surviving pottery kiln in Britain.

Not all pottery used in Somerset was made here. Earthenwares from north Devon, Bristol, probably

Part of a hoard of 275 silver crowns, half-crowns and shillings found in East Street, Taunton. The date of the latest coins shows the hoard to have been buried at the time of one of the sieges of Taunton which took place in October 1644 and April-May 1645.

broke out. There is evidence that the ditches of Taunton and Bridgwater Castles were re-cut and probably widened to put them in a state of defence. A good earthwork bastion survives at Taunton superbly sited to cover the town bridge with artillery and parts of the earthwork defences on the east side of the town have been located by archaeological excavation. Earthworks behind the Luttrell Arms may be part of the siegeworks erected to invest Dunster Castle. Invaluable service as a stronghold for the Parliamentarian cause did not prevent Taunton Castle suffering the fate of all the other castles – being rendered indefensible by demolition and slighting after the Civil War had fully ended. A Civil War coin hoard recovered from East Street, Taunton, is a reminder of how traumatic these times were.

Silver locket found on the site of the Battle of Sedgemoor. It depicts King Charles II on one side and his queen, Katherine of Braganza, on the other. The locket, which is 20mm in height, presumably belonged to a soldier loyal to James II.

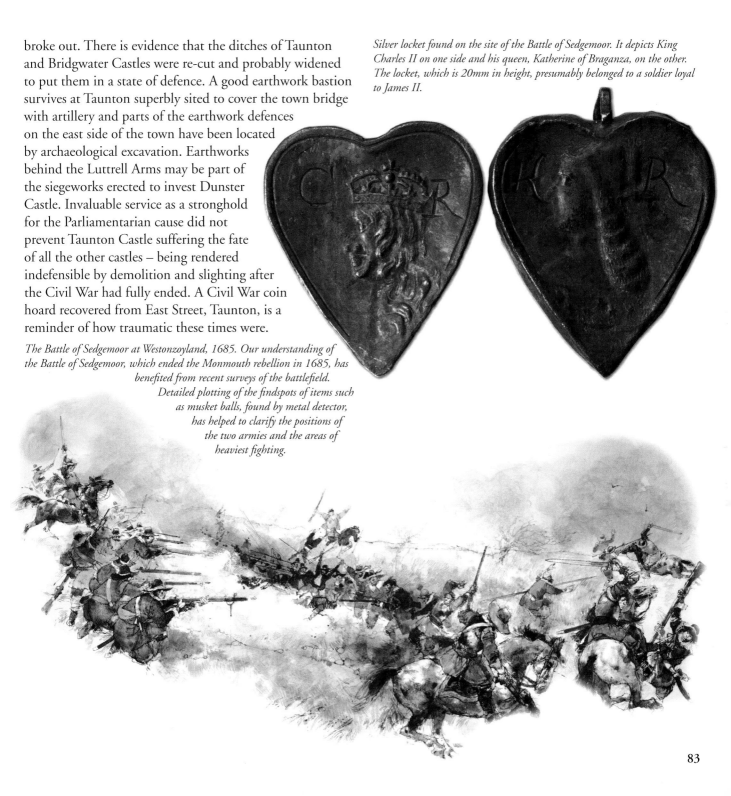

The Battle of Sedgemoor at Westonzoyland, 1685. Our understanding of the Battle of Sedgemoor, which ended the Monmouth rebellion in 1685, has benefited from recent surveys of the battlefield. Detailed plotting of the findspots of items such as musket balls, found by metal detector, has helped to clarify the positions of the two armies and the areas of heaviest fighting.

The Industrial Age

Introduction

William Blake's memorable evocation of 'dark satanic mills' seems inappropriate when describing the effects of the Industrial Revolution in Somerset. In 1700, travelling conditions made the county remote from both the metropolis and the embryonic crucibles of the Revolution in the Midlands and the North. Somerset also lacked the resources in depth to sustain growth and production over the length of time, and at the levels later experienced elsewhere. But from *c.* 1750 to *c.* 1914 a series of new technologies had a major impact on urban and rural landscapes, leaving a range of sites and structures for subsequent industrial archaeologists to record. These include the linear incisions of the burgeoning transport infrastructure of the period, opening or improving routes for the distribution of King Coal and much else besides.

The county had already experienced an expanding economy during the 17th century and when Daniel Defoe was observing Somerset's prosperous woollen industry in the 1720s the Darbys were still developing their iron furnaces at Coalbrookdale. Allied to industrially-driven initiatives was the movement for agricultural improvement. Numerous and far-reaching changes, begun before 1700 and continuing well after 1800, meant that agriculture, paradoxically, remained Somerset's principal industry. The benefits of improved agriculture were promoted locally by the pioneering efforts of John Billingsley of Shepton Mallet and others, while the Royal Bath and West of England Society was chief among the organisations which provided a forum for enlightened members of the farming community and for manufacturers of such items as soil conditioners and iron implements. In the countryside, improvements achieved by the late enclosures (1794–1820) were matched in importance by schemes for draining the wetlands. Here (from 1830 onwards) pumps and engines, most notably by Easton, Amos and Anderson, brought the application of steam power to a problem that had hitherto lacked an effective technology.

Extraction

The county's diverse geological strata continued to ensure a supply of building stone with a variety of colours and textures, the traditional quarries producing items such as kerbs, paving and quoins. The Carboniferous limestone and basalt of Mendip, however, having been recognised as high-quality road stones, gave rise to quarrying on a vastly different scale, assisted by the new rail network, which the quarries themselves helped to ballast. William Beauchamp (est. 1867) and later John Wainwright were two major quarrying firms that responded to ever-increasing demand.

Lime kilns, Somerset's most numerous industrial monuments, played a seminal role in providing burnt lime for building purposes and for neutralising acid soils. Kilns of the draw type were fuelled by culm, a Welsh anthracite. They have front arches which are predominantly scalloped-shaped in western Somerset but triangular in the east, with some evidence surviving for lean-to shelters (as at Vallis Vale) and inclines to the tops of the bowls (as at Doniford). The Jurassic Lower Lias allowed the production on a more industrial scale of quick-setting, hydraulic cement and Blue Lias lime, with banks of kilns as at Dunball, Langport, Pylle, Shepton Mallet and Watchet. John Board sought to perfect an improved Portland cement alongside the traditional Roman version, and exhibited ornamental cement figures at the Great Exhibition of 1851.

Early small-scale slate working is known at Chibbet Ford, Combe and Rook's Castle, but three larger quarries exploited the relatively poor-quality Devonian Morte series in competition with slate from Delabole (Cornwall) and north Wales. Investors included the Dean and Chapter of Wells at Oakhampton near Wiveliscombe, and the Trevelyans of Nettlecombe Court at Treborough on the Brendon Hills, roofing slates, lintels and hearths being produced. At Tracebridge, near Ashbrittle, the slate was sold for damp-proofing courses with cut and finished rock for water troughs and dairy slabs. Gypsum, found chiefly at Blue Anchor, was converted to plaster of Paris or carved as alabaster into funeral monuments and Victorian tourist souvenirs. At Cannington, pink and white barytes was quarried to a depth of 30 feet from 1916 to *c.* 1921. The hand-digging of peat turf for fuel continued into the 20th century but was substituted by machine-cutting to supply the profitable gardening and horticulture markets.

During the 19th century there was a renewed search for minerals in the upland regions, adits and shafts often being located at or near the 'ancient workings' of earlier miners. Partners of the Ebbw Vale ironworks formed the Brendon Hills Iron Ore Company in 1853, settlements growing up around mines at Gupworthy and Raleigh's Cross, together with mining structures such as Burrow Farm engine house. A trade recession and imported Spanish ore brought closure in 1879 with only a brief revival later (1907–10). Over Exmoor, iron and copper mining was sporadic with mines principally at Cornham Ford, Eisen Hill and Wheal Eliza. Copper mining on the Quantock Hills reached an intensive phase between *c.* 1790 and *c.* 1825 when two structures at Dodington shared a Boulton and Watt beam engine.

The engine house at the Glebe shaft of the Dodington copper mines, built in 1820.

Limekiln at Doniford in about 1910. One of the large number of kilns built to burn lime for building and also associated with agricultural improvement. They cluster, not surprisingly, on limestone bedrock but also along the coast where they could obtain lime and coal by sea.

The retort house at Kilve. Part of a short-lived attempt to obtain oil from the shale rock, which was soon proved to be uneconomic.

Interior of J W Singer and Sons of Frome, England's leading art foundry during the late 19th century and (left) one of their bronze castings, The Sluggard, c. 1890.

The failure to find deeper reserves of lead ore on Mendip led to the reworking of earlier slags and tailings (from *c.* 1830 to *c.* 1908) and caused furnaces, condensing flues, buddles and other structures to be erected on the former Chewton and Priddy mineries. At Charterhouse on Mendip, where features have been recorded in detail, silver was recovered using the Pattinson process. Calamine (zinc carbonate) was mined extensively for the Bristol brass industry (from *c.* 1600 until *c.* 1850) leaving areas of 'gruffy' ground around Shipham. The seasonal mining of ochre at Axbridge, for use as pigments and for sheep marking, necessitated the construction of a trammed inclined plane.

Geological faulting and folding posed difficulties for coal mining, but the introduction of steam engines for pumping and winding (1750–1830) resulted in about 90 working collieries in historic Somerset. Improvements in mechanisation, ventilation and transport encouraged further growth until c. 1900 when creeping

ELEVATION OF BRIDGWATER·BRIDGE

CAST ANNO 1795 AT COALBROOK DALE

The iron bridge at Bridgwater (1797) replaced the Medieval stone bridge with a single span.

rationalisation began the process of closing uneconomic pits and signalled the end of small family-run operations. Two other potentially important industries, started by drilling boreholes, failed to develop. A coal prospecting venture at Dunball (1909–10) discovered salt suitable for both table and industrial purposes; a small works was in operation until 1922. In 1924 a retort was erected at Kilve to extract crude oil by the breaking of shale, but its sulphur content, and the need to mine as well as quarry, brought about the project's early curtailment.

Manufacturing

Somerset's own Ironbridge – the Coalbrookdale-cast, 75-foot span across the Parrett at Bridgwater (1797) – was symbolic both of a new age and the special contribution of metal processing. By the 1830s local foundries, using bar iron from south Wales, were exerting their influence on everyday life. Some were synonymous with agricultural machinery (Day of Mark and Dening of Chard) and the Fussells, at their six edge-tool works around Mells,

were renowned for hay knives, reap hooks and the like. The Phoenix Works (Chard) produced pumps and road-making equipment, whilst Singer (Frome) specialised in ornamental bronze and ironwork (for example, Boudicea's statue at Westminster Bridge). Since many industries were still located along watercourses, iron wheels and gearing, replacing wood, made a great difference, especially for the many corn and farm mills.

After about 1850 founders like William Sparrow and George Parsons (both of Martock) added a new dimension by supplying portable or stationary steam engines to supplement or replace water (and occasionally wind) power and, more fundamentally, to allow the relocation of workplaces or the creation of new ones where water was secondary to the availability of coal. Emerging water and gas utilities not only provided sources of power, but also work for founders who cast mundane parts like pipes and drain covers. The infant electricity companies opted for a variety of generating plants including steam engines (Taunton, 1886), suction gas engines (Minehead, 1902), turbines (Brushford, 1906) and waterwheels (Porlock, 1909). At Yeovil a continuous transition was made from cast-iron stoves at the Nautilus Works to Petter oil engines and, finally, engineered aircraft and helicopters.

Archaeologically, the early 18th-century woollen industry is difficult to trace, the many processes being at dispersed sites. By the 1770s competition from outside Somerset was felt amongst the coarse-serge makers of Bridgwater and Taunton, but later also affected Shepton Mallet and Frome. At Wellington, the united families of the Weres and Foxes, and their neighbours the Elworthys at Westford, successfully introduced the centralised and mechanised factory system. Silk and crepe manufacture continued a textile tradition (at Taunton and Darshill, Shepton Mallet) as did bobbin net (machine lace) at

Beam engine used for powering silk machinery in Taunton from 1865-1955. It is now in the Somerset County Museum, Taunton.

Chard. From *c.* 1870 cotton, in the form of collar-making, appeared notably at Taunton and Ilminster. In South Somerset flax and hemp were essential fibres in twine, rope, webbing and sailcloth (the last equipping Nelson's navy) with mills and 'walks' being located at Crewkerne, Dowlish Ford, Merriott and North and West Coker. Castle Cary gained a long-lasting reputation for horsehair products under the guidance of Thomas Matthews and John Boyd (from *c.* 1820 onwards). Hand papermaking with rags at 'batch' mills (Fideoak) became a 19th-century casualty with the introduction of continuous processes (as at Wookey).

Brewing flowed from the inn-based brewhouse to the brewery, a structure that could be sizeable and ornate (as at Shepton Mallet). Similarly, the small rural malthouse using local barley (as at Lynch) grew into large maltings (Oakhill). Amalgamations and takeovers were the norm, a typical example being Starkey, Knight and Ford (est. 1895) which had origins in Bridgwater, Burnham on Sea, North Petherton and Tiverton.

Animal products spawned town and country tanneries ranging in size and scale from Thomas Poole's at Nether Stowey to the later complexes of Clark, Son & Morland and Baily at Northover, Glastonbury, which included manufacturing. Nearby at Street the Clark's leather dressing and shoemaking interests resulted in the building of a model town. Yeovil became the centre of the glove industry that, despite relying on outworkers, established factories there and at Milborne Port, Stoke sub Hamdon and Tintinhull.

Curiously, the two most familiar products of Somerset – cider and Cheddar cheese – remained, until the 20th century, in the farmhouse and dairy, although Highbridge once held two cheese markets a week and a bacon factory was built (1890) to accept pigs fattened on whey.

Easily won clay deposits and good communications were critical locational factors for the heavier end of the pottery industry and by 1800 Bridgwater was dominant, with lesser centres later at Bishops Hull, Glastonbury, Highbridge and Yeovil. Lucrative and widely-distributed items included Dutch-styled pantiles, perforated malt kiln tiles, Bath bricks

Harry Frier's view of Starkey, Knight and Co's brewery in Taunton. In the 19th century there were often significant industrial works in town centres. The sewing machine shop by the bridge is still there.

(made from the River Parrett's siliceous slime) and (from *c.* 1840) land-drainage pipes. Kiln technology developed from temporary, coppice-fired clamps to intermittent types like the updraught (Blue Anchor), downdraught (Somerset Brick and Tile Museum) and finally the continuous firing Hoffmann kilns, three being built at West Buckland. Despite the construction of the semi-automated Chilton Trinity Tile Factory (opened 1930), manual skills remained a characteristic of the industry.

Until the 1930s pottery vessels continued to service the domestic, horticultural and small-holdings markets, the most long-established potters working in the vicinity of Donyatt. Many brickworks offered decorative and practical ceramics. John Browne, a Bridgwater manufacturer, housed his kilns inside a former glass cone, the relic of an unsuccessful early 18th-century venture by the first Duke of Chandos.

TRANSPORT

Locally-crewed ships often sailed to the four corners of the British Empire, but most commercial traffic concerned itself with the coastal trade of the Irish Sea and the Bristol Channel. Of the ketches, schooners, trows and other wooden sailing vessels that visited harbours along

Somerset's coastline many were from local shipyards, Bridgwater accounting for over 130 during the 18th century. Minehead Quay had been constructed and extended by George Luttrell of Dunster Castle in the 17th century, while Porlock Weir was improved by Col. G W Blathwayt some

200 years later. Watchet had to be extensively remodelled following the gales of 1900 and 1903, which also caused the abandonment of the Acland-Hood family's harbour at Lilstock. Difficulties were also experienced by larger ships sailing upriver to Bridgwater, and offloading took place at Combwich until

The opening of the Bristol and Exeter Railway through Somerset in 1841-4 was followed by other railways and led to a significant change in the availability of mass-produced goods and greater potential for travel.

Porlock Weir in the1890s. The harbour is pictured at low tide and contains sloops, ketches and fishing boats. The fish market was situated opposite the Anchor Hotel.

the town's docks, which gave refuge from the Parrett's bore and silt, were opened in 1841. Close to the river's estuary at Dunball, wharfs were established in 1844 and there was a similar but much older facility at Highbridge.

Inland navigation on one of the Parrett's tributaries, the Tone, had been improved under an Act of 1699 and the half locks installed functioned sufficiently well until the 1820s when trade transferred to the Bridgwater and Taunton Canal. Grand plans during the 'canal mania' of the 1790s, which projected waterways across Somerset, were drastically truncated. The resulting canals and river canalisations were mainly completed in the 1840s, coinciding with the arrival of the railways. Two canals, the Grand Western (Somerset section 1838–68) and the Chard (1842–67), designed for the use of 26-foot tub-boats, required relatively unusual engineering features including inclined planes, boat lifts and tunnels.

The setting up of turnpike trusts constituted the first concerted effort since Roman times to provide and maintain a system of main roads in Somerset. Thirty trusts, set up under Acts of Parliament, had routes within the county's boundaries. Bridgwater was one of the earliest (1730) but most of the other trusts first appeared between 1752 and 1759. Toll houses, of which about 70 are still extant, had a board of charges (as at South Cheriton) and a gate (as at Brutasche Terrace, Street). Architectural styles varied to include the single storeyed (for example Muchelney), the semi-hexagonal (Eastham's Gate, Merriott) and the converted cottage (Hemington). Although waning by the 1860s, the trusts did make a significant contribution to the development of the county's road network, including the creation of some lengthy sections of new road (Honiton and Ilminster Trust's 1807 route towards Devon) and of shorter but important connections (Bridgwater Trust's Bridgwater to Pawlett road, 1822).

Carriageways were generally upgraded, a benefit of the presence of J L McAdam and his relatives as surveyors for several trusts, although Thomas Telford's more expensive form of road construction continued until the 1930s. Many bridges had been the responsibility of the County Justices at Quarter Sessions since 1555 but transport-related developments brought major structural alterations. Some medieval bridges were bypassed (such as Haselbury Old Bridge in 1830), while others were rebuilt entirely (Great Bow Bridge, Langport, 1840–1), occasionally overcoming local topographical difficulties (Murder Combe, 1790). Bridgwater founders contributed with cast ironwork.

Ambitious rail schemes were rejected or modified by intense entrepreneurial competition, which created an uncoordinated network: Wells and Yeovil each having three stations. Through routes were favoured by the companies later to be incorporated into the Great Western Railway. The Bristol and Exeter, opened between 1841 and 1844, was the first with an impressive engineering work, Whiteball Tunnel at the Devon Boundary. To the east was the Wiltshire, Somerset and Weymouth (1850–6), but a connecting line to London, from Durston to Castle Cary, came much later (1905–6). The influence of I K Brunel can be seen in lineside architecture (Bridgwater and Frome stations) and originally in the broad rail gauge (7 ft 0 in), the final conversion occurring in 1892.

The Somerset and Dorset did eventually make it possible to travel coast to coast, passengers alighting from paddle steamers at Burnham on to a stone pier (built 1858), with Poole, Dorset as an eventual destination. The company's Mendip route south from Bath (1874) proved especially challenging with three imposing viaducts in the vicinity of Shepton Mallet. By the mid-1870s most main and branch lines were in operation, some being distinctive for the commodities carried such as strawberries on the Cheddar Valley and Yatton (1869–70) or iron ore on the West Somerset Mineral Railway (1856–64), descending from the Brendon Hills to Watchet down a 1:4 incline. Additionally there were sidings for industrial concerns like timber yards or pastoral ones like milk-collecting depots and short internal works tramways mainly serving the extractive industries. Through the provision of travel excursions the railways had a profound effect on people's lives, truly uniting the population of Somerset by 'the iron'.

THE ARCHAEOLOGY OF THE RECENT PAST

INTRODUCTION

It may seem strange to consider the archaeology of recent times, but this is a growing area of research and analysis. Archaeological techniques are being increasingly used in police investigations to recover information from crime scenes, particularly burial sites, but this is peripheral to archaeology's general aim of studying the past through material culture.

In the Palaeolithic a single flint may form the only evidence and be intensively studied, but in more recent times the research focus broadens and many areas of human activity are hardly considered. This is particularly marked as we approach the present day, partly because of the wealth of written and illustrative material that exists for the 19th and 20th centuries, but also because of the interests of researchers. In the 19th century, for example, the focus is on industry, with much less effort being expended on the domestic sphere. Redevelopment of a factory may merit archaeological recording work, but archaeologists routinely dig away the remains of houses to get to earlier deposits. The factory speaks to us of a different age, but many still live in familiar Victorian homes.

In the 20th century the focus is almost exclusively on military archaeology, a reflection of its exotic nature, current interest as important anniversaries pass, and the sudden redundancy of very recent structures following the end of the Cold War.

MILITARY ARCHAEOLOGY OF THE EARLIER 20TH CENTURY

Little remains of Somerset's role in the First World War, which, in fact, left few archaeological traces in England as a whole. The county was primarily used for training at places such as at North Hill, Minehead, and Victorian barracks, such as Jellalabad in Taunton, continued in use. It is likely that more sites, such as the Remount Centres that supplied replacement horses to the military, will be identified.

Somerset's training role continued in the inter-war years with the anti-aircraft gunnery range at Doniford and its associated airfield at Westonzoyland (active from 1925). The county's first airfield, however, had been established at Yeovil in 1917, next to the Westland factory. Preparations for the coming war only really started in 1938 when the Admiralty began looking for training sites in the county, leading to the establishment of RNAS Yeovilton. Events moved fast and two years later Somerset was facing the very real threat of invasion.

ANTI-INVASION DEFENCES OF THE SECOND WORLD WAR

The suddenness of the German success in western Europe, which saw them in control of the north coast of France in June 1940, produced an emergency programme of defence construction in Britain to counteract the invasion threat. There was not enough equipment to defend every beach and so a system of defence lines was conceived inland. This was based on the General Headquarters (GHQ) Line that ran from Burnham on Sea eastwards, round London and then north towards Scotland. From behind this line, it was hoped, the army could deploy to wherever the enemy threatened. In front of the line the land

Contemporary plan of the defences proposed for the anti-tank island at Forton. The plan gives a good impression of the scale of the defences built in addition to the pillboxes. As can be seen from the blue pencil, not all the plans were carried out.

Pillbox on the Taunton Stopline at Creech St Michael. The pillbox was originally on the railway embankment, which has been lowered to reveal its foundations, and contributed to the defences where the line joined the Bridgwater and Taunton Canal.

was crossed by subsidiary "stoplines" whose aim was to slow an invasion and allow time for the counter attack.

Apart from the GHQ line, two lines crossed Somerset, the Ringwood West line, running south from the GHQ line near Frome, and the Taunton stopline, which ran from the west end of the GHQ line to the south coast at Axmouth and was intended to contain an invasion in Devon or Cornwall. All the lines were constructed to impede the progress of the combined tank and infantry forces that the Germans had used to such effect in France. Defences were based around a linear anti-tank obstacle, which where possible, use pre-existing features. The Taunton stopline followed the River Parrett, the Bridgwater and Taunton Canal, the Chard Canal, the railway, and the River Axe.

The GHQ line similarly followed the River Brue before crossing country to the join the Kennet and Avon Canal at Bradford on Avon. Where no existing feature was suitable, a ditch was dug about 5m wide and 3m deep, and where this was not possible, lines of concrete cubes 1.5m high were used. These were covered by fire from troops in concrete emplacements, known as pillboxes. In front of the line would be minefields, and bridges which crossed the line were prepared for demolition. It is estimated that over 1000 pillboxes were constructed in Somerset in a few months in late 1940, part of over 18,000 constructed nationwide. As each took about 100 tonnes of concrete the logistical arrangements to achieve this are remarkable. The works were planned by the military but civilian contractors, for example Stansells of Taunton, were employed in the construction work that included disguising the pillboxes in various ingenious ways.

No sooner was work underway than the strategy of stoplines was abandoned as it was realised that there were not enough troops to man linear defences and a new doctrine of defended localities (known as anti-tank islands) was introduced. Defences similar to those on stoplines were constructed on all sides of towns and road crossings. Manning these required fewer troops and each would have to be captured by an enemy force – again slowing it down to allow a counter attack.

Although Somerset's beaches face north, they were also defended against both hit-and-run attacks and the possibility of a German attack launched from Ireland, whose neutrality was suspected. The coastal defences are far less well preserved than the stop lines as most have been cleared to improve holiday resorts. Recent work around Minehead and Dunster has shown that there are two phases of defence present but, so far, no documentary evidence has been found to explain this.

AIRFIELDS

Airfields are the largest features to remain from wartime Somerset and some are still in use. The ruins of Westonzoyland will be well-known to travellers between Bridgwater and Langport, but others, such as RAF Culmhead or RNAS Charlton Horethorne, will be less familiar.

RAF Culmhead survived in remarkable condition until the late 1990s, as it continued to be used as a radio station, but since that closed, many of the buildings have

Defended wall at the rear of one of the fighter pens at RAF Culmhead. The airfield was extremely well defended on the western side for reasons that are not clear.

been demolished. Two areas, however, have been legally protected as Scheduled Monuments because of the elaborate defences against ground attack on the west side of the airfield. Culmhead also saw the introduction of the first jet aircraft into RAF service.

DEFENCES AGAINST SHIPS AND AIRCRAFT

After the first invasion panics it was decided to re-establish the Victorian defensive line across the Severn, and the old battery on the end of Brean Down was rebuilt to house two 6-inch guns. These were housed in concrete emplacements that can still be seen, together with concrete bases for the corrugated-iron Nissen huts which housed the large garrison. Similar constructions can be seen on Steep Holm.

Anti-aircraft artillery has left fewer visible remains, although some of those defending Bristol can be seen to the north of Mendip. Apart from at Barwick, to the south of Yeovil, all the known sites in Somerset were for mobile guns without concrete emplacements and the physical remains of such sites, as with searchlight batteries, are likely to consist of Nissen hut bases from accommodation. A good example, including flat earthen platforms for guns and lights (previously interpreted as a prehistoric settlement!) has recently been identified on the Quantocks.

Radar sites are similarly rare in the county, but one can be seen on North Hill, Minehead, which operated in a dual anti-ship and anti-aircraft role. Fragmentary remains survive of a Ground Controlled Interception (GCI) station at Long Sutton, used to guide fighter aircraft to their targets.

A more unusual site is the bombing decoy on Black Down near Shipham, one of a number surrounding Bristol. Such sites were intended to mimic bombing targets at

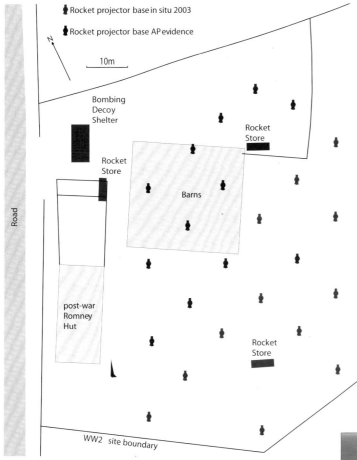

Plan of the rocket battery to the south of Black Down. Based around one of the bunkers for the bombing decoy, the rockets were inaccurate and would all have been launched at once to produce a shot-gun effect. Some of the concrete bases for the projectors (as the launch equipment was known) were fitted with cast-iron compass rings (above).

night and thus to lure enemy bombers to drop their bombs in open country. Black Down was designed to replicate the railway layout of Bristol, with lights suggesting signals and the glow from coalfired locomotives. The troops manning the decoy were provided with protected bunkers from which to control the site. Once attacked, fires could be lit to simulate the burning city and to attract further bombers. The site also has the remains of lines of earth and stone mounds which were erected earlier in the war to prevent invasion aircraft landing. These lines are a rare survival since, despite being erected in many places elsewhere, they were usually soon cleared to permit farming. The Black Down examples survive because of the military use of the area for the decoy, but they have become confused in local memory as the streets of the 'decoy town'.

Brean Down coast artillery battery. The fixing for one of the six-inch guns can be seen on the left with ammunition lockers to the right. In the background is the other gun house – both were originally roofed to protect from air attack.

CIVIL DEFENCE

The civilians of Somerset were not in the same danger as those in the south-east or in industrial areas. Nevertheless, attacks were made on targets such as the Westland Factory in Yeovil and there was always danger from hit-and-run raiders or bombers returning from raids on Bristol or south Wales. Few remains of civil defence installations can be seen in Somerset. A few domestic shelters survive in gardens, and communal shelters are visible in several areas of Yeovil. Another rare survival is what appears to be the site of an emergency water tank (for fire-fighting) in the car-park of the King's Arms in Taunton where a circular groove in the concrete would have held the tank walls.

Musgrove Park hospital (seen here in 1944) was one of a number built during the Second World War in the Taunton area that played an important part in treating the large numbers of American casualties resulting from the Normandy landings.

Training

Several areas of Somerset were used for training including the ranges at Doniford, mentioned already. Much training took place on Exmoor where an extensive artillery range was established. Tank training was undertaken on North Hill, Minehead, where, despite post-war attempts at clearance, roads, target rails and protective bunkers can still be seen. At the east end of the hill the ramps used to unload tanks from lorries survive in the woods close to the radar station mentioned above. The ranges at Yoxter, on Mendip, are still in use.

D-Day

Somerset took an active part in the allied landings in Normandy, particularly in sending out airborne troops from Westonzoyland, but also in being the main area for returning casualties. Most of the troops involved were American whose activities are poorly documented in British records. Huge ammunition dumps were established by the roadside in eastern Somerset and large numbers of troops were billeted in preparation. Hospitals were built around Taunton and Yeovil, including Musgrove Park, which continues in use. Merryfield airfield was equipped with a field hospital for immediate treatment of air-lifted casualties and a blood bank was established in Chilton Polden.

The Cold War

With the end of the Second World War Soviet Russia was quickly perceived as the new danger. With the introduction of long-range missiles and bombers, most places in Britain were now under a similar level of threat.

A new network of radar stations was established (the Rotor programme) with one at West Myne above Minehead. The siting of this station occasioned heated debate as it lay on National Trust Land and construction was only permitted following design changes to make the buildings more acceptable. Rapid advances in radar made the site redundant only a few years later and led to its almost complete removal. Such was the secrecy surrounding the site that only one (recently declassified) photograph is known and no plans have been located.

The Royal Observer Corps transferred from its wartime work of aircraft reporting to one of recording and reporting nuclear attacks. To facilitate this role, a network of underground bunkers was established in the years around 1960, 22 of which were in Somerset. The Somerset bunkers reported to a Group Headquarters in Yeovil, which is one of the best-surviving in the country.

RNAS Yeovilton was also modified at this time to allow V-bombers, carrying nuclear weapons and normally stationed in eastern England, to disperse here in times of crisis. The runway was strengthened and lengthened for these large aircraft and a separate area established in the south of the air station for the bombers and their crews.

The Royal Observer Corps Group Headquarters at Yeovil. Partly underground and sealable against contamination, the group headquarters would have collected information on nuclear weapons detonations from smaller monitoring posts and used it to assess the scale and location of attacks.

PLACES TO VISIT

PALAEOLITHIC AND MESOLITHIC

The remains of these early periods, when few or no structures were made, are obviously limited to portable objects from caves and other deposits. The gravelly foreshore at Doniford, near Watchet, where A L Wedlake found many Palaeolithic handaxes and flakes, is open to the public and still produces occasional finds. The Middle Palaeolithic occupation site at the Hyaena Den can be visited during a tour of the Wookey Hole Caves and objects from here can be seen in the small museum in the old paper mill. For those interested in the Upper Palaeolithic period, Gough's Cave and its excellent museum are well worth a visit, especially during the winter when there are fewer tourists. The Early Mesolithic cave burial site at Aveline's Hole is accessible from the road running through Burrington Combe, but is potentially dangerous and should only be approached with extreme caution. Displays of Palaeolithic and Mesolithic finds can be seen in several local museums, notably Wells and Mendip Museum, the Market House Museum in Watchet, and Somerset County Museum in Taunton.

NEOLITHIC AND BRONZE AGE

The most common and visible monuments of these periods are barrows. The most impressive groups are the Priddy Nine Barrows and the nearby Ashen Hill group which can be seen from a footpath. The Priddy Circles are just to the north but lie on private land. Many barrows, hut circles and stone settings can be visited on Exmoor (see *The Field Archaeology of Exmoor* under General Reading). The Ebbor Gorge nature reserve contains rock shelters occupied during these periods. The Peat Moors Centre at Westhay has reconstructions of prehistoric trackways and Somerset County Museum in Taunton has many displays of artefacts from the Neolithic and Bronze Age including the South Cadbury Shield, trackways and other finds from the Somerset moors.

IRON AGE

Hillforts and other ditched and banked enclosures provide the most visible evidence for the Iron Age. They occur across the county and range from the dramatic and imposing sites of Ham Hill and Cadbury Castle in the south-east, to smaller structures further west such as Brent Knoll (rising above the Levels), Plainsfield Camp and Trendle Ring (Quantock Hills), and Bats Castle and Cow Castle (Exmoor). Many of these sites involve a strenuous walk but the benefit, besides a visit to the site, is often a spectacular view.

An insight into life in the Iron Age can be gained by a visit to the Peat Moors Centre at Westhay where the reconstructions include houses based upon the excavations at Glastonbury Lake Village. The Centre also features the excavation site hut used by Arthur Bulleid and Harold St George Gray throughout their excavations at Meare Lake Village between 1908 and 1956.

Glastonbury Lake Village Museum in High Street, Glastonbury, displays some of the most important finds from the excavations but most material is held at the Somerset County Museum, Taunton, notably the finds from Cadbury Castle and Ham Hill. Also worth a visit is the Camelot Inn, South Cadbury, where a display tells the story of the site and where refreshments can be enjoyed after the steep walk up to the hilltop and walk around the ramparts.

ROMAN

Somerset has surprisingly little of its Roman past on view today. At Charterhouse on Mendip the low earthworks of the fort are visible to the north-east of the Charterhouse Centre, the settlement earthworks being in Town Field across the valley. To the east, the large rakes in the nature reserve are probably the result of Roman mining, although much of the area has been altered subsequently. Nothing of Roman Ilchester, nor any villas, are on view but Somerset County Museum in Taunton, the Museum of South Somerset in Yeovil, and Ilchester Museum have good displays.

BRITONS AND SAXONS

South Cadbury and Glastonbury Tor are both accessible to the fit, and well worth the climb, but there is nothing visible of this date at either site. In historic Somerset, to the south of Bath, the Wansdyke is visible in several places and the Saxon church in Bradford on Avon (just over the border in Wiltshire) is one of the best examples in the country. The church at Milborne Port shows the best evidence for possible Saxon craftsmanship within the county and the plans of the halls at Cheddar have been marked out in concrete in the school grounds. The excavated material from South Cadbury can be seen in Somerset County Museum.

MEDIEVAL

In contrast to earlier periods, there is a wealth of surviving Medieval sites to visit. Most villages, for example, contain a Medieval church and all are worth visiting. There are also monastic ruins at Glastonbury, Cleeve and Muchelney and the Cathedral at Wells. The most accessible deserted Medieval settlements are at Ramspits on Mendip and Nether Adber in South Somerset and close to the latter is the moated manor site at Marston Magna. A motte and bailey castle can be visited at Nether Stowey, as can stone-built castles at Dunster, Farleigh Hungerford and Nunney. Examples of Medieval town planning can be seen at Chard, Wellington, Montacute, Glastonbury and Wells, settlements which also contain surviving Medieval buildings. The fine Late Medieval George Inn at Norton St Philip is also worth visiting.

POST-MEDIEVAL

Many of the features and monuments mentioned in the text are available to be studied and enjoyed and there are many more examples throughout Somerset. Many early industrial sites have been obliterated by later industrial development but the pottery kiln at Dunster, carefully conserved by Exmoor National Park, is an exception. The scale of the enclosed landscape and engineering structures such as King's Sedgemoor Drain still impress. Somerset County Museum contains the principal exhibition of Post-Medieval material, particularly pottery and the Butler collection of cauldrons and skillets, but there are also exhibits in Bridgwater (both at the Blake Museum and Somerset Brick and Tile Museum), Chard and Wells. Somerset Rural Life Museum in Glastonbury and Watchet Boat Museum also contain exhibits. Although later in date, they reflect the forms of agricultural equipment and boats from this pre-industrial age.

INDUSTRIAL

Sites and structures of the industrial age can be found throughout Somerset and most museums touch upon aspects of the county's working past, for example, Chard and District Museum which has displays on agricultural engineering and the machine net lace industry. The power of water and steam is demonstrated at Dunster Castle Mill and Westonzoyland Pumping Station respectively, and the Bridgwater & Taunton Canal, together with the West Somerset Railway, have also benefited by full restoration. On Exmoor and Mendip it is still possible to trace in safety the impact of mining on the landscape. The remains of the lead industry lie all around the car park at Charterhouse. A handbook to 500 of the more important surviving monuments, *Somerset's Industrial Heritage: A Guide and Gazetteer* (1996) has been edited by Derrick Warren and contains information on accessibility.

MODERN

The fabric of the twentieth century can, obviously, be seen all around us but specific remains of military activity are more widely spread. The defences of the GHQ line and Taunton stopline can be seen at many places along their route and are most accessible along the Bridgwater & Taunton Canal. Airfields can be seen at Westonzoyland and limited amounts of Culmhead are visible from the bridleway. RNAS Yeovilton remains in use but also contains the Fleet Air Arm Museum. The battery at the end of Brean Down is in the care of the National Trust and the area of the bombing decoy on Black Down is also accessible. Numerous Royal Observer Corps posts survive, some still cared for by former members. The best is perhaps at Snowdon Hill, Chard, where an earlier Orlit post survives together with its underground replacement.

FURTHER INFORMATION

SOMERSET HISTORIC ENVIRONMENT RECORD

The SHER, which incorporates the Somerset Sites and Monuments Record (SMR), is a computerised register of known archaeological and historic sites in the county. Each site record contains a précis of published and unpublished information about the site together with its location. The database is searchable in many ways, including by period, site type, parish, and national grid reference, and forms the basis of many types of research. It can be searched over the Internet or information can be sent by post or email in response to queries. Personal visits are also welcome but it is appreciated if an appointment is made.

Address: The Somerset Historic Environment Record
          Taunton Castle, Castle Green
          Taunton, TA1 4AA.
Call: 01823 424040
Email: heritage@somerset.gov.uk
Website: www.somerset.gov.uk/heritage

SOMERSET COUNTY MUSEUMS SERVICE

Somerset County Museums Service is the primary archaeological archive for Somerset. It provides care for and access to material from excavations, fieldwork and chance finds from all periods and from all over Somerset. Personal visits are welcomed but a minimum of two week's notice is recommended to ensure that the relevant reference collections can be made available.

Address: Somerset County Museum
          Taunton Castle, Castle Green
          Taunton, TA1 4AA
Call: 01823 320200
E-mail: county-museums@somerset.gov.uk
Website: www.somerset.gov.uk/museums

PORTABLE ANTIQUITIES SCHEME

Archaeological objects such as pottery, flint and metalwork are frequently found in the county in a variety of ways, for example by metal detectorists, gardeners or people out walking. Such discoveries, individually or cumulatively, can add significantly to our knowledge of the past. The Somerset and Dorset Portable Antiquities Scheme exists to encourage people to report their finds for identification and recording purposes. To report an archaeological find or to learn more about the Scheme contact the Finds Liaison Officer at:

Address: Somerset County Museum
          Taunton Castle, Castle Green
          Taunton, TA1 4AA
Call: 01823 320200
Email: county-museums@somerset.gov.uk

FINDS OF TREASURE

The law on Treasure has been revised and the definition clarified. In general terms Treasure includes all objects of gold or silver over 300 years old but excludes single coins. Recently, prehistoric hoards of any metal have been included in the definition. Finds of Treasure must be reported to the Coroner who will hold an inquest if a museum is intested in acquiring them. Otherwise they are disclaimed and returned to the finder. If claimed, there is usually a reward equal to the market value. Objects of potenial Treasure must be reported within 14 days of discovery. This can be done through the Portable Antiquities Scheme (see above), which can also give preliminary advice.

Somerset Archive and Record Service

The Somerset Archive and Record Service exists to find, preserve and make available the records of the historic (pre-1974) county of Somerset. Holdings comprise many millions of documents spanning more than 1000 years of Somerset history, and every year some 10,000 researchers visit the service's headquarters at the Somerset Record Office in Taunton. Collections include the great estate archives of Somerset's landed families, official collections such as the records of Quarter Sessions, parish collections, private and business records, and thousands of printed and manuscript maps: such sources are essential for understanding the history of Somerset individuals, communities and landscapes. The service's website includes an on-line catalogue giving access to 300,000 catalogue descriptions.

    Address: Somerset Record Office
              Obridge Road
              Taunton, TA2 7PU
    Call: 01823 278805
    Email: archives@somerset.gov.uk
    Website: www.somerset.gov.uk/archives

Somerset Archaeological and Natural History Society

The Somerset Archaeological and Natural History Society has a programme of lectures and excursions, and publishes an annual volume of Proceedings and a twice-yearly newsletter. It also has a large private library (see Somerset Studies Library), where members have direct access and are able to borrow books.

    Address: Somerset Archaeological and
              Natural History Society
              Taunton Castle, Castle Green
              Taunton, TA1 4AA
    Call: 01823 272429
    Email: office@sanhs.org
    Website: www.sanhs.org

Victoria County History of Somerset

The Victoria County History of Somerset exists to research, write and publish the history of Somerset parish by parish. The first volume appeared in 1906, a further six have been published and four more are in the press or in preparation. In addition to the published volumes the VCH maintains a library of research notes and materials used to prepare both completed parish histories and those that have yet to be compiled.

    Address: Victoria County History of Somerset
    Address: Somerset Record Office
              Obridge Road
              Taunton, TA2 7PU
    Call: 01823 278805
    Email: archives@somerset.gov.uk
    Website: www.somersetpast.net

Somerset Studies Library

The Somerset Studies Library, on the first floor of Taunton Library, has reference copies, and other Somerset libraries have lending copies, of most of the published books and articles on Somerset archaeology. The Somerset Studies Library also has microfilm copies of tithe maps, and large-scale Ordnance Survey maps and vertical air photographs, all covering most of the county. The Somerset Archaeological and Natural History Society's large private library is in the next room, and contains complete sets of most British archaeological journals. Non-members may have these fetched, but do not have direct access to the society's shelves. The library is open six days a week, and no appointment or evidence of identity is needed.

    Address: Somerset Studies Library, Paul Street
              Taunton, TA1 3XZ
    Call: 01823 340300
    Email: somstud@somerset.gov.uk
    Website: www.somerset.gov.uk/libraries

FURTHER READING

In addition to the works cited, much has been published by the Somerset Archaeological and Natural History Society (SANHS) in their annual *Proceedings* (from 1851), which can be consulted in libraries both in Somerset (Bath, Burnham, Bridgwater, Chard, Frome, Keynsham, Midsomer Norton, Minehead, Nailsea, Street, Taunton, Wells, Weston super Mare and Yeovil) and further afield. The *Proceedings of the University of Bristol Spelaeological Society* contain many papers on topics related to the Mendip area and some local societies also produce reports. The Somerset Studies Library has copies of most.

GENERAL

The present book is the third to be called *The Archaeology of Somerset*. The first was Dina Dobson's pioneering work in 1931. This was followed by Michael Aston and Ian Burrow's volume in 1982. Lesley and Roy Adkins' *Field Guide to Somerset Archaeology* (1992) gives details of many of the more visible sites (although it should be noted that some of these are on private land).

More up-to-date surveys of several Somerset themes can be found in *Somerset Archaeology* edited by Chris Webster in 2000. This is now out of print but can be downloaded from www.somerset.gov.uk/heritage. Other works which cover important topics in the county include the two excavation reports on South Cadbury: Leslie Alcock, *Cadbury Castle, Somerset: The Early Medieval Archaeology* (1995) and John Barrett and others, *Cadbury Castle, Somerset: The Later Prehistoric and Early Historic Archaeology* (2000). Exmoor has recently been authoritatively covered by Hazel Riley and Rob Wilson-North in *The Field Archaeology of Exmoor* (2001) as have the Quantock Hills by Hazel Riley, *The Historic Landscape of the Quantock Hills* (2006). Somerset features in the wider-ranging *The Archaeology of South West England* edited by Chris Webster (2007).

PALAEOLITHIC AND MESOLITHIC

The most recent and reliable survey of the Lower and Middle Palaeolithic periods in Britain is John Wymer, *The Lower Palaeolithic Occupation of Britain* (1999). For the Upper Palaeolithic and Mesolithic periods, good general accounts can be found in Christopher Smith, *Late Stone Age Hunters of the British Isles* (1992) and Nicholas Barton, *Stone Age Britain* (1997). More detailed accounts of the archaeological evidence from Somerset are contained in the works under General.

NEOLITHIC AND BRONZE AGE

The best coverage of these periods is given in *The Archaeology of South West England* (see under General) but there is also more detailed coverage of some topics. The stone settings, roundhouses, barrows and field systems on Exmoor form an important part of *The Field Archaeology of Exmoor* (see under General). The wetland archaeology of the Somerset Levels is summarised in Bryony and John Coles, *Sweet Track to Glastonbury* (1986) and there are overviews of Somerset barrows by Leslie Grinsell in *SANHS Proceedings* 113 (1969) and 115 (1971). The Somerset County Museums Service has published a well-illustrated account of the *South Cadbury Shield*. General studies of the period include John Coles and Anthony Harding, *The Bronze Age in Europe* (1979), Julian Thomas, *Rethinking the Neolithic* (1991) and Richard Bradley, *The Social Foundations of Prehistoric Britain* (1984).

Iron Age

The standard work of reference for the period is the fourth edition of Barry Cunliffe's *Iron Age Communities in Britain* (2005). More general introductions to the subject are Barry Cunliffe's *Iron Age Britain* (1995) and *Britain and the Celtic Iron Age* by Simon James and Valery Rigby (1997). The Iron Age in the west of the county is well covered in *The Field Archaeology of Exmoor* (see under General). There are several site-specific publications, including the Cadbury Castle report (see under General) and two books on the lake villages by John Coles and Stephen Minnitt, *Industrious and Fairly Civilized: The Glastonbury Lake Village* (1995) and *The Lake Villages of Somerset* (2006).

Roman

The Roman period in Somerset has recently been expertly reviewed by Peter Leach in *Roman Somerset* (2001) and the same author has also published the important excavations at Ilchester and Shepton Mallet: *Ilchester Volume 1: Excavations 1974–75* (1982), *Ilchester Volume 2: Archaeology, Excavations and Fieldwork to 1984* (1994), and *Shepton Mallet – Fosse Lane: Excavations of a Romano-British Roadside Settlement at Shepton Mallet* (2001). The history of Roman Britain is covered by Peter Salway, *The Oxford Illustrated History of Roman Britain* (1993) and Sheppard Frere, *Britannia* (1987). The effects of the Roman empire are covered by Martin Millett, *The Romanization of Britain* (1990) and a good survey of the later period is Simon Esmond Cleary's *The Ending of Roman Britain* (1989).

Britons and Saxons

The literature on the early post-Roman period is large and much needs to be treated with caution if the depths of Arthur-mania and modern 'celtic' mysticism are not to be plumbed. The Cadbury Castle report (see under General), together with Philip Rahtz and others, *Cannington Cemetery* (2000) and Warwick Rodwell, *The Archaeology of Wells Cathedral: Excavations and Structural Studies 1978–93* (2001) cover the most important sites in the county. A good general work is Barbara Yorke's *Wessex in the Early Middle Ages* (1995) and others include those by Ken Dark, *Civitas to Kingdom* (1994) and *Britain and the End of the Roman Empire* (2000), and Nick Higham, *Rome, Britain and the Anglo-Saxons* (1992). John Blair's *The Church in Anglo-Saxon Society* (2005) covers this important topic and also discusses wider issues.

Medieval

Somerset's Medieval archaeology was reviewed in Mick Aston's *Aspects of the Medieval Landscape of Somerset* (1988) and in his and Carenza Lewis's *The Medieval Landscape of Wessex* (1994). There is a vast amount of historical information collected in the *Victoria County History of Somerset* volumes (see under Sources) and Clare Gathercole and Miranda Richardson reviewed all the Medieval towns in the *Somerset Urban Archaeological Surveys* (unpublished, but copies available in libraries and on-line at www.somerset.gov.uk/heritage). A summary of ten years' work on Shapwick has been produced by Mick Aston and Chris Gerrard, 'Unique, Traditional and Charming: The Shapwick Project 1989–99', *Antiquaries Journal* 79, (1999), 1–58; the full report will be published shortly. Monasteries have been covered by Robert Dunning, *Somerset Monasteries* (2000) and Mick Aston, *Monasteries* (1993), while Warwick Rodwell has covered Wells Cathedral in *The Archaeology of Wells Cathedral: Excavations and Structural Studies 1978–93* (2001). Robert Dunning has written the history of *Glastonbury* (1994) and there is a more archaeological study by Philip Rahtz and Lorna Watts, *Glastonbury* (2003).

POST-MEDIEVAL

A good general overview of Post-Medieval archaeology is provided by David Crossley, *Post-Medieval Archaeology in Britain* (1990) and Richard Newman, *The Historical Archaeology of Britain c. 1549–1900* (2001). References specific to work in Somerset are scattered, but the journal *Post-Medieval Archaeology* provides a useful starting-point. Key excavations are Richard Coleman-Smith and Terry Pearson, *Excavations in the Donyatt Potteries* (1988) and Peter Leech, *The Archaeology of Taunton: Excavations and Fieldwork to 1980* (1984), with John Allan's *Medieval and Post-Medieval Finds from Exeter 1971–1980* (1984) as the comparator external sequence. There is a further useful summary of Somerset pottery by John Allan in *Somerset Archaeology* (see under General). Roderick Butler and Christopher Green have published their research in *English Bronze Cooking Vessels and their Founders 1350–1830* (2003) and '*... fire burn and cauldron bubble': English Bronze Cooking Vessels.* (2006). Two surveys published by the Royal Commission on the Historical Monuments of England are significant: Roger Leech, *Early Industrial Housing: The Trinity Area of Frome* (1981) and Christopher Stell, *An Inventory of Non-Conformist Chapels and Meeting-houses in South-West England* (1991). Jane Penoyre, *Traditional Houses of Somerset* (2005), illustrates some of the Post-Medieval changes to building design in the county.

INDUSTRIAL

An instructive introduction to the development of industrial archaeological studies in the county is given in Brian Murless's chapter in *Somerset Archaeology* (see under General). Angus and Sandy Buchanan cover Somerset in their *Industrial Archaeology of Central Southern England* (1980), which gives a good indication of the diversity and spread of industries. More detailed studies of smaller areas include Robin Atthill's seminal *Old Mendip* (1971) and *Exmoor's Industrial Archaeology* (1997) edited by Michael Atkinson. Canals and railways have generated a plethora of literature with road heritage faring less well, the exception

being *Somerset Roads* in two volumes (1985 and 1987) by John Bentley and Brian Murless. The publications of the Somerset Industrial Archaeological Society provide a core source, reflecting the dedication of its members, which can be consulted at the Somerset Studies Library and have been drawn upon extensively in an overview by Peter Stanier, *Somerset in the Age of Steam* (2000) which also contains a useful, subject-orientated bibliography.

RECENT PAST

The best overview of the Second World War in Somerset is Mac Hawkins, *Somerset at War* (1996). There are more detailed treatments of the GHQ line in Colin Alexander *Ironside's Line* (1999) and Martin Green *Warwalks: Stop Line Green* (1999). Don Brown covers events on Mendip, particularly the role of the British resistance units, in *Somerset v Hitler* (1999). The Council for British Archaeology has produced a series of reports by Colin Dobinson, *Twentieth Century Fortifications in England* which cover all the main types of archaeological remains; they are unpublished but there is a set in the SANHS library. Dobinson has also written two published books based on the reports: *Fields of Deception: Britain's Bombing Decoys of World War II* (2000) and *AA Command: Britain's Anti-Aircraft Defences of the Second World War* (2001); further books are planned. The CBA also produces a very useful handbook to aid identification, edited by Bernard Lowry, *20th Century Defences in Britain: An Introductory Guide* (1998).

ACKNOWLEDGEMENTS

Many people have helped to bring this book to publication. We are especially grateful to Professor Mick Aston for providing the Foreword, to the Publications Group of Somerset County Council, chaired by Rachel Boyd, and to Steven Pugsley. In addition we thank Lawrence Bostock, who has designed the book with such skill, and John French who worked on the digital images. Steve Minnitt has provided essential editorial help, as has Mary Siraut, who also prepared the index. David Bromwich, Somerset Studies Librarian, has as always been unfailingly helpful. We are very grateful to Victor Ambrus for creating many of the reconstruction drawings used in the text. James Montgomery has kindly allowed the use of the reconstructions by Jane Brayne relating to Cadbury Castle. The originals can be seen in the Camelot Inn, South Cadbury. Chris Norman would like to thank Roger Jacobi for his comments on chapter two.

The majority of the illustrations are reproduced from the collections of Somerset County Council's Heritage Service. For permission to use other illustrations the following are gratefully acknowledged:

Victor Ambrus, 20 (above), 52 (above left), 54 (above), 64, 83 (below)

Ashmolean Museum, Oxford, 61

Jane Brayne, cover illustration, 58

The British Museum, 20 (below right), 21 (inset)

John Coles, 33

David Dawson, 82 (above)

Frome Museum, 86 (above right)

GSB Prospection, 42 (above), 72 (lower right, detail)

Alan Graham, 71 (left)

Frances Griffith and Devon County Council, 28 (left)

English Heritage, 21 (main), 27, 35, 53, 88

Tom Mayberry, 11 (right), 16 (below), 60 (below), 61 (above), 79 (above), 93

Edward Mortelmans, 29

The Natural History Museum and Andy Currant, 19 (main)

Chris Norman, 20 (below left), 24

Stuart Prior, 31 (above)

Jane Reed, 63 (below left)

Somerset Archaeological and Natural History Society, 7, 9, 11 (above), 11 (below left), 12, 13, 40, 45, 52 (above right), 62 (left), 65 (main), 66, 69, 70 (above), 71 (right), 72 (above), 75, 76, 78, 87, 89, 90

Somerset Levels Project, 26, 30, 37